Classic English
MEDALLION STYLE
QUILTS

BETTINA HAVIG

American Quilter's Society
P. O. Box 3290 • Paducah, KY 42002-3290
www.AQSquilt.com

To Charlotte
Best Wishes –
Alaskan Cruise
2004
Bettina Havig

I

Located in Paducah, Kentucky, the American Quilter's Society (AQS) is dedicated to promoting the accomplishments of today's quilters. Through its publications and events, AQS strives to honor today's quiltmakers and their work and to inspire future creativity and innovation in quiltmaking.

EDITOR: BARBARA SMITH

GRAPHIC DESIGN: ELAINE WILSON

COVER DESIGN: MICHAEL BUCKINGHAM

PHOTOGRAPHY: CHARLES R. LYNCH, QUILT PHOTOS.
      BETTINA HAVIG, PAGES 7, 9, 12, 15, 18, 19, 29, 51, 55, 88, 110
      KAY B. SMITH, PAGES 4, 20, 21, 23, 27, 33, 35, 39, 41, 59, 63,
            65, 69, 73, 77, 79, 85, 103

Library of Congress Cataloging-in-Publication Data

Havig, Bettina
    Classic English medallion style quilts / Bettina Havig
        p. cm.
    ISBN 1-57432-829-8
    1. Patchwork--Patterns.   2. Quilting--Patterns.   I. Title

    TT835.H3483   2003
        746.46'041--dc22

                    2003017688

Additional copies of this book may be ordered from the American Quilter's Society, PO Box 3290, Paducah, KY 42002-3290; 800-626-5420 (orders only please); or online at www.AQSquilt.com. For all other inquiries, call 270-898-7903.

Dedication

To my husband, Alan, and my daughter, Kirsten, who always encourage and support my quiltmaking.

Acknowledgments

Without the machine quilting skills of Kim Diamond, whose machine quilting helped bring the quilts to life, I would never have been able to complete nine quilts in a year.

Dorothy Olser, with her clear and deliberate analysis of British quilts, brought the frequently used elements of construction into focus.

My editor, Barbara Smith, who was patient with my stubbornness and enthusiasm for the quilts, guided the project through its final stages.

Contents

Introduction

Through a long-standing interest in both the history of quiltmaking and a fascination with the English quilt tradition, I developed a workshop on classic English medallion quilts. The quilts in this book are the result of the fun I had in developing samples for the workshop, plus a few other pieces.

Within the English tradition, the more proper name for this style might be "framed quilts" in reference to the sequence of framing borders used in their construction. The term "medallion" has settled into our contemporary quilt vernacular. Most of us understand what is meant by a medallion quilt, that is, a quilt with a central motif surrounded by a sequence of borders. The center of the classic medallion quilt is completely discretionary, with no prescribed size or style. It may be pieced, appliqué, *broderie perse*, or perhaps a single commemorative textile.

A classic English medallion quilt is specific in the contributing elements. The border units adhere to a small group of prevalent pieced components. Ten of these units are illustrated on pages 10–19. By using only those units most common to the traditional English medallion quilts,

you can generate considerable variety. Among the components that appear frequently in early English framed quilts are Sawtooth, Hour Glass, Double and Triple Squares, Bars, Flying Geese, Framed Squares, Uneven Nine-Patch, and Evening Star. For the projects, you will primarily be cutting squares of 2", 3½", and 6½" to construct these units for the borders. Any exceptions will be noted in your project.

THIS BOOK IS DIVIDED INTO THREE SECTIONS:

1. The basic instructions for the border elements or units that will be used repeatedly in the construction of the projects

2. Plans for specific quilts ranging from crib- to full-sized bed quilts, including patterns and suggestions for the medallion centers when applicable

3. A do-it-yourself design section, complete with charts to help you plan your medallion-style quilts

In every case, the choice for the center focus of the medallion is open to variation. If you like, you can substitute a different block of the same size for your quilt. Take some liberties and have some fun. For example, you could use any 15" pieced or appliqué block in the place of the Arrowhead block in the quilt titled WIGGLESWORTH on page 22.

It is assumed that you know basic quilt construction for finishing your English medallion quilt.

THE NAMES OF THE QUILT PROJECTS ARE TAKEN FROM WHIMSICAL PLACE NAMES THAT ACTUALLY EXIST IN BRITAIN. I TRAVEL BY CAR WHEN VISITING THERE, AND SO I SCOURED MY "BRITISH ROAD ATLAS" FOR PLACE NAMES FOR THE QUILTS. BELIEVE IT OR NOT, MUGGLESWICK ACTUALLY EXISTS IN THE NORTHEAST OF ENGLAND, IN COUNTY DURHAM.

Seated: Amy Emms, who was honored by the queen as a Member of the British Empire (MBE), made important contributions to the continuation of quiltmaking in England. Standing: Dianne Huck (left), editor of *British Patchwork and Quilting Magazine*, with author Bettina Havig. The photo was taken just weeks before Amy died.

Before You Start

Generally, in English medallion quilts, you will find that each pieced border is preceded and followed by a border cut from whole cloth with no piecing. These strip borders act as spacers and help make the transition to measurements that will accommodate whole-number repeats of units for the next pieced border. The measurements for these borders are given in each pattern.

Instructions for constructing all the border units used in the quilt projects are given on pages 10–19. Refer to these instructions as you create the units indicated for your chosen project. Measure the units as you make them to confirm that they are the predicted size. As you add each border to your quilt, check your results with the measurements given in your project. Think of it as checking the gauge as you might if knitting a sweater.

Fabric Selection

The quilts are designed with multiple fabrics and are intended to have a scrappy look. Variations in the distribution of the fabrics will make the quilt more your own creation. The number of units needed are given, but the precise placement of each fabric is up to you. Extra yardage is provided with that flexibility taken into consideration — depending on how you choose to place fabrics, you may find that you need more of some and less of others.

If you find you are short of a fabric, do as our foremothers did. Incorporate an additional fabric choice into the plan. As long as the new fabric is compatible, the addition will actually enhance the quilt.

THEME

Begin by selecting a theme or focal fabric. This is the fabric most visible in the quilt. You will see it repeatedly, sometimes in the piecing and usually in the strip borders, which keep the quilt moving outward. The theme fabric is an important initial choice. It sets the palette for the quilt. For best results, choose a medium- to large-scale, multicolored print. It doesn't have to have an English look. Any fabric that appeals to you will work.

BACKGROUNDS

In addition to the theme fabric, you will usually need background fabric. Often background prints are neutral, but that does not mean they must be wimpy. I suggest choosing two or more background fabrics. Vary the scale and color slightly. Be a little daring and select a background that has a large-scale print but a neutral color.

MIXERS

Finally, you need to select the indicated number of additional fabrics. These are "mixers" from which you will piece the border units in conjunction with the theme and background prints. This group of fabrics should be compatible with your theme fabric. Use the theme fabric as a guide and make it the arbiter of the palette. The mixers should be small to medium in scale and have relatively low contrast with each other. For example, these might all fall into the medium to medium-dark values, or they could be all pastel or all light to medium light in value. Don't be afraid to select more fabrics than indicated. The given amount represents the minimum number of mixer fabrics.

Planning Charts

There is a planning chart for each pattern so that you can easily substitute same-sized units to create your own distinctive borders. The charts provide the finished size of each unit along with the border's addition to the overall quilt size. While the precise number of pieces are listed for each pattern, you may want to cut a few extras to leave some options open in the arrangement of the units.

The size of the center block of each quilt is given, and rotary cutting instructions (or templates, if needed) are also given for that block. You can substitute any pieced, appliquéd, or *broderie perse* block that you desire so long as it is the same size as in the original plan.

I hope you enjoy making these framed, or medallion-style, quilts.

ONE OF THE MANY VERY NARROW STREETS WHICH ONE CONFRONTS WHEN DRIVING IN ENGLAND

English Medallion Units

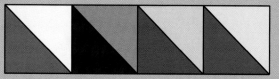

BARS, PAGES 11–12

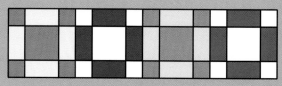

HOUR GLASS, PAGE 15

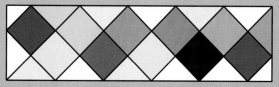

DOUBLE SQUARES, PAGE 13

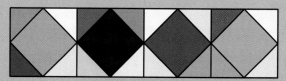

FRAMED SQUARE, PAGE 16

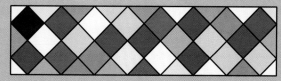

TRIPLE SQUARES, PAGE 13

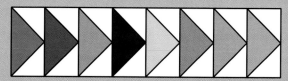

FLYING GEESE, PAGE 17

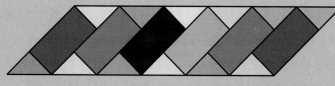

SAWTOOTH, PAGE 14

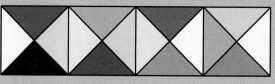

UNEVEN NINE-PATCH, PAGE 18

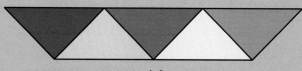

DOGTOOTH, PAGE 14

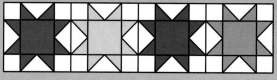

EVENING STAR, PAGE 19

Basic
Unit Construction

Two sizes are given for several of the units. Measurements for the larger size are given in parentheses. Use ¼" seam allowances for all units and border seams.

BARS, DOUBLE AND
TRIPLE SQUARES

There are many possible variations of these border units. The key is that they contain multiple squares, offset by one square as they are joined, or that the bar used is equal to a multiple of squares; for example, two, three, or more squares.

The finished bar strips will measure 3⅛" wide (3⅝" including seam allowances).

TO MAKE BAR UNITS, CUT:

one 3½" square
two 2" x 3½" bars

1. Cut the 3½" square diagonally twice to make four quarter-square triangles. Note that the triangles are slightly oversized.

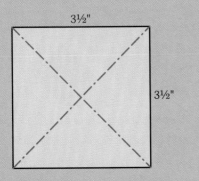

2. Sew triangles to both ends of each bar, as shown, and trim off the points.

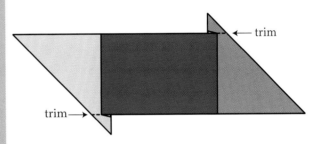

3. Arrange the bar units in a row, offsetting them by half a bar.

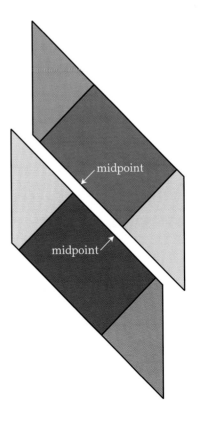

English Medallion Units

A COUNTRY "KIRK" OR CHURCH NEAR BROMS-
GROVE, WORCESTER

4. Sew the bar units together. Press and trim, leaving ¼" seam allowances beyond the points. The finished width of the border is 3⅛".

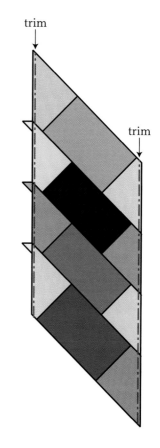

5. For each corner, sew a bar corner-turning unit (described on page 13).

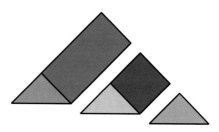

English Medallion Units

Double Squares. You can create double-square units by substituting two 2" squares sewn together in place of the 2" x 3½" bar. The finished result will be the same size.

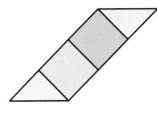

Make a double-square turning unit for each border corner.

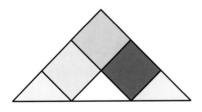

Triple Squares. Use three 2" squares for a triple-square unit. This border finishes 4¼" wide.

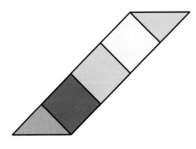

Make a triple-square turning unit for each corner.

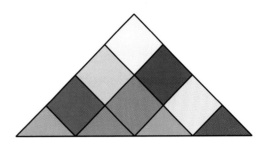

Corner-turning Units

Bars, double squares, and triple squares are joined in sequence, leaning in one direction. Depending on which direction the units lean, you will add the corner-turning unit on the end that will complete the border strip. Sew the strips to the quilt and join the border strips at the corners with mitered seams.

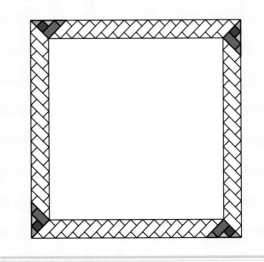

English Medallion Units

SAWTOOTH

The Sawtooth unit should measure 3⅛" (6⅛") square, including its seam allowances.

TO MAKE SAWTOOTH UNITS, CUT:

two 3½" (6½") squares

1. Cut the two squares in half diagonally to make four half-square triangles.

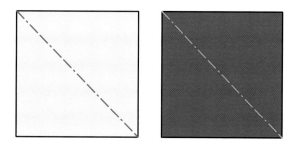

2. Pair triangles of different fabrics. Match the right angles to align them, then sew the diagonal edges together. Be careful to avoid stretching the pieces. The Sawtooth finishes 2⅝" (5⅝").

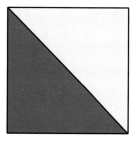

Note: Measurements in parentheses are for making a larger unit.

DOGTOOTH

The Dogtooth border will finish 1⅛" (2⅝") wide, and 2¼" (5¼") on the long side of triangle.

TO MAKE DOGTOOTH TRIANGLES, CUT:

two 3½" (6½") squares

1. Cut the squares diagonally twice to make eight quarter-square triangles.

2. Sew the triangles together in strips, alternating colors. Trim off the "dog ears."

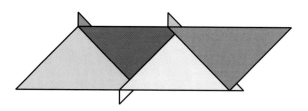

Designing Borders Tip

When designing your own borders, use the finished measurements in the following figure to determine the number of units you will need. (The numbers in parentheses are for the larger unit.)

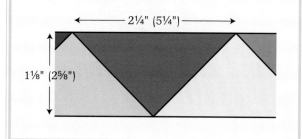

English Medallion Units

HOUR GLASS

The Hour Glass unit should measure 2¾" (5¾"), including seam allowances.

TO MAKE HOUR GLASS UNITS, CUT:

four 3½" (6½") squares

1. Cut the four squares twice diagonally to make 16 quarter-square triangles.

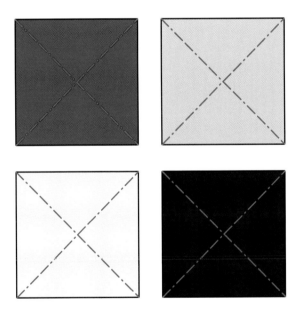

2. Join triangles in pairs of different fabrics. Press seam allowances to one side.

3. Join pairs of triangles to form the Hour Glass unit. The unit finishes 2¼" (5¼").

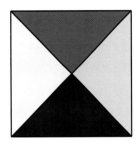

THIS IS THORNBURY HOUSE BED AND BREAKFAST HOTEL WHERE THE AUTHOR STAYED WHILE IN THE MALVERN AREA.

English Medallion Units

FRAMED SQUARE

The Framed Square should measure 3½" (6½") square, including its seam allowances.

TO MAKE FRAMED SQUARES, CUT:

one 3½" (6½") square
four 2" (3½") squares

1. With the right sides of the fabrics together, sew a small square, along its diagonal, to each of two opposite corners of the large square.

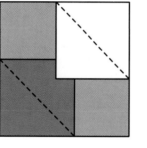

2. Trim the excess fabric away at each corner, leaving ¼" seam allowances.

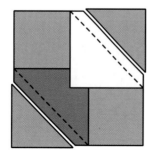

3. Press the two triangles back.

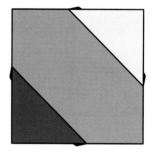

4. As before, sew smaller squares to the other two corners. Trim and press to finish the unit, which finishes 3" (6").

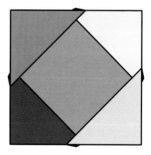

Framed Square Tip

Framed Squares can be chain sewn by sewing opposite diagonals before trimming and pressing.

English Medallion Units

FLYING GEESE

Flying Geese should measure 1¾" x 3" (3¼" x 6"), including seam allowances.

TO MAKE FLYING GEESE, CUT:

one 3½" (6½") square
four 2" (3½") squares

1. Make a Framed Square as described on page the preceding page.

2. Align your ruler with the center square's diagonal and cut the Framed Square in half to make two Flying Geese units.

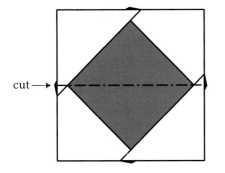

cut →

3. Rotate one of the Flying Geese and realign them as shown.

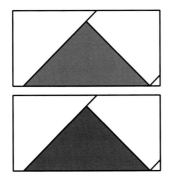

4. To create borders, sew units together in groups of four to six.

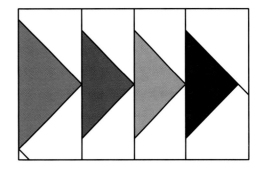

5. Trim off the excess fabric, leaving ¼" seam allowances beyond all the points, except the last unit. Press the seam allowances away from the points. The unit finishes 1¼" x 2½" (2¾" x 5½").

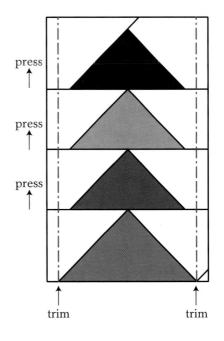

press
press
press
trim   trim

English Medallion Units

UNEVEN NINE-PATCH

The Uneven Nine-Patch should measure 6½", including seam allowances.

TO MAKE UNEVEN NINE-PATCHES, CUT:

> one 3½" square
> four 2" squares
> four 2" x 3½" bars

1. Join the squares and bars into three strips as shown. Press seam allowances toward the darker fabric.

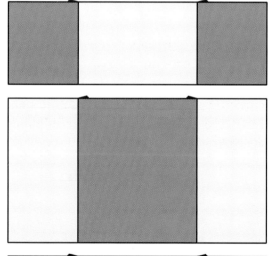

2. Join the three strips. Press to the outside edge of the unit, which finishes 6".

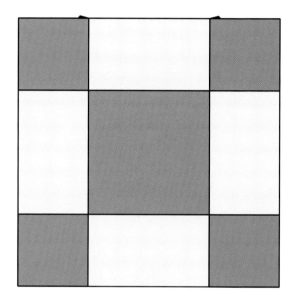

THIS NORMAN HOUSE NEAR CAMBRIDGE (THE MANOR, HEMINGFORD GREY) BELONGS TO DIANA BOSTON, THE DAUGHTER-IN-LAW OF LUCY BOSTON, A FAMOUS ENGLISH AUTHOR AND PATCHWORKER. THE HOUSE IS OPEN TO TOURS BY APPOINTMENT.

English Medallion Units

EVENING STAR

The Evening Star should measure 4½" (6½"), including seam allowances.

TO MAKE EVENING STARS, CUT:

STAR FABRIC
> one 2½" (3½") square
> four 1⅞" (2⅜") squares

BACKGROUND
> one 3¼" (4¼") square
> four 1½" (2") squares

1. Cut the four 1⅞" (2⅜") squares on one diagonal to make eight half-square triangles for the star points.

2. Cut the 3¼" (4¼") square on both diagonals to make four quarter-square background triangles.

3. Join background and star pieces into three strips as shown.

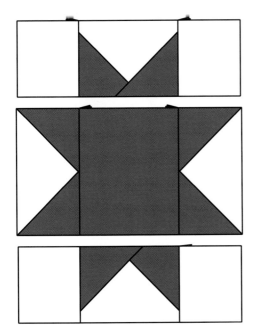

4. Join the three strips to complete the Evening Star unit.

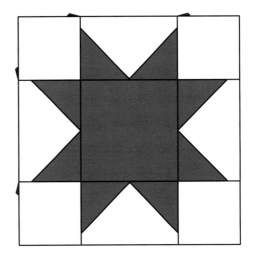

You now know how to make all of the border units used in the patterns and are ready to start your project. The projects begin on page 22, or you can jump to page 86 to begin planning your own medallion-style quilt if you prefer.

THE NEEDLE MUSEUM IN REDDITCH

Medallion Quilt Patterns

PICCADILLY CIRCUS, LONDON

WINDOW DISPLAY, FORTNUM & MASON, LONDON

ABOVE: TRAIN STATION AT BATH SPA

WEST FRONT TOWERS OF WESTMINSTER ABBEY, LONDON

TOURIST INFORMATION

VICTORIA COACH STATION

BUCKINGHAM PALACE

QUEEN'S GALLERY ROYAL MEWS

VICTORIA

STREET SIGN IN LONDON

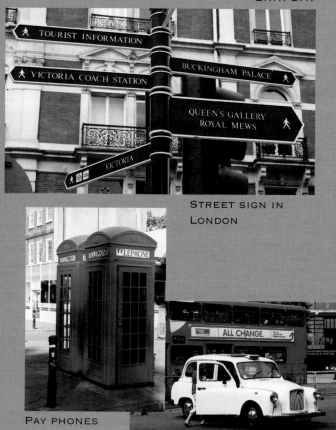

PAY PHONES

TAXI

FLOWERS ABOVE THE SARACENS HEAD TAVERN, BATH

ABOVE: DETAIL OF THE PRINCE
ALBERT MEMORIAL, LONDON
LEFT: ROYAL MAIL BOX

FLORAL CROWN CELEBRATING THE QUEEN'S
GOLDEN JUBILEE IN THE CENTER OF A TURN-
ABOUT IN BATH, ENGLAND

BIG BEN, NAME OF THE BELL IN THE CLOCK TOWER
RISING ABOVE THE HOUSES OF PARLIAMENT

Wigglesworth (44" x 44"), by the author; machine quilted by Kim Diamond

EACH BORDER TREATMENT DEPENDS ON THE ACCURATE CUTTING AND PIECING OF THE PRECEDING BORDERS. USING ¼" SEAM ALLOWANCES IS CRITICAL. AS YOU WORK, VERIFY THE QUILT'S DIMENSIONS AFTER EACH PIECED BORDER HAS BEEN ADDED AND, IF NECESSARY, MAKE ADJUSTMENTS TO THE NEXT STRIP BORDER TO BRING THE QUILT INTO COMPLIANCE WITH THE SIZE CALCULATED.

Fabric Requirements

FABRIC	YARDS
1 theme (all strip borders)	1½
7 mixers	½ ea.
2 lt. backgrounds	1 ea.
Backing	3
Binding	¾
Batting	50" x 50"

Reserve the theme fabric needed for all strip borders before cutting patches.

THE VICTORIA AND ALBERT MUSEUM IN LONDON IS THE WORLD'S LARGEST MUSEUM OF DECORATIVE ARTS.

Wigglesworth

CENTER BLOCK

The center of the medallion is an Arrowhead block. You can substitute any 15" (15½" with seam allowances) block of your choice.

Referring to the block assembly diagram and using the following cutting instructions, make the Arrowhead block.

THEME
 1 A 4¼" x 4¼"
 4 B Use the pattern on page 27.
 2 D 5" x 5", cut diagonally twice to make 8 quarter-square triangles

MIXERS (4 EACH OF 3 FABRICS)
 12 E 2⅜" x 2⅜"

BACKGROUND
 4 C 2¾" x 2¾", cut diagonally once to make 8 half-square triangles
 1 D 5" x 5", cut diagonally twice to make 4 quarter-square triangles
 24 E 2⅜" x 2⅜"

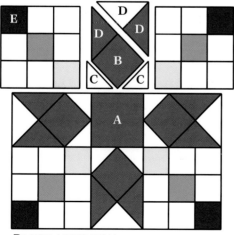

BLOCK ASSEMBLY

BORDER ASSEMBLY

Referring to the quilt assembly diagram (page 25) and the cutting instructions for each border, add the following five borders in sequence.

BORDER 1. STRIP

THEME
 2 strips 2" x 15½"
 2 strips 2" x 18½"

Border 1 adds 3" and the quilt measures 18½" square.

BORDER 2. FRAMED SQUARE

Follow the instructions on page 16 to make 28 Framed Squares in the 3" size (3½" with seam allowances).

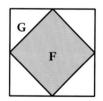

MIXERS
 28 F 3½" x 3½"

BACKGROUND
 112 G 2" x 2"

Border 2 adds 6" and the quilt measures 24½" square.

Wigglesworth

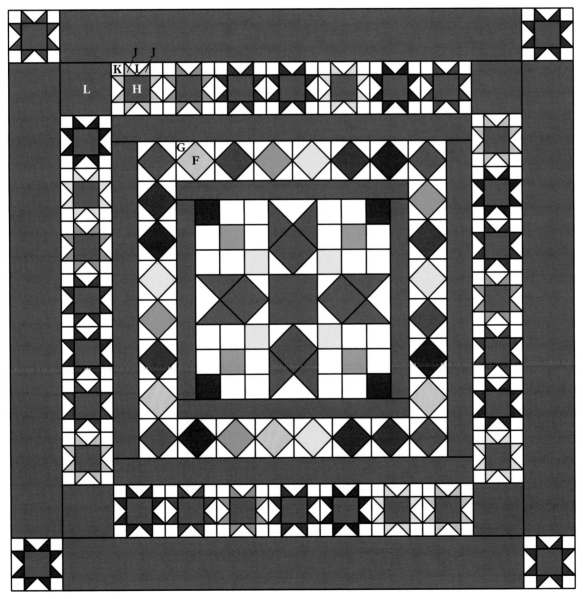

QUILT ASSEMBLY

Wigglesworth

BORDER 3. STRIP

THEME

> 2 strips 2½" x 24½"
> 2 strips 2½" x 28½"

Border 3 adds 4" and the quilt measures 28½" square.

BORDER 4. EVENING STAR

Refer to page 19 to make 32 of the 4" Evening Stars (4½" with seam allowances). Four of the stars will be used in the corners of Border 5.

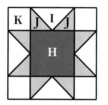

THEME

> 32 H   2½" x 2½" star centers
> 4 L   4½" x 4½" border corners

MIXERS (IN SETS OF 4)

> 128 J   1⅞" x 1⅞", cut diagonally once to make 256 star points

BACKGROUND

> 32 I   3¼" x 3¼", cut diagonally twice to make 128 side triangles
>
> 128 K   1½" x 1½" corner squares

Border 4 adds 8" and the quilt measures 36½" square.

BORDER 5. STRIP

THEME

> 4 strips 4½" x 36½"

Add an Evening Star to each corner when attaching the border strips.

Border 5 adds 8" and the quilt measures 44½" square.

FINISHING

Layer the quilt top, batting, and backing. Baste and quilt the layers. Medallions can be simply and effectively quilted with grid or outline stitching.

Use your favorite technique to bind the layers. The binding yardage is sufficient for any method, including double-fold or bias binding.

PLANNING CHART

Use the construction and planning chart on page 97 to substitute same-sized units or to add borders to your quilt. See Planning Your Own Quilts on page 86 for detailed information on determining the number of units to use in a border and the width of spacer strips.

Wigglesworth

ABOVE: DETAIL OF THE VICTORIA AND ALBERT
MUSEUM BUILDING IN LONDON
BELOW: ALBERT MEMORIAL BUILT IN 1876 BY
QUEEN VICTORIA TO HONOR PRINCE ALBERT

B

Wigglesworth

Muggleswick

Muggleswick (68" x 68"), by the author; machine quilted by Kim Diamond

EACH BORDER TREATMENT DEPENDS ON THE ACCURATE CUTTING AND PIECING OF THE PRECEDING BORDERS. USING ¼" SEAM ALLOWANCES IS CRITICAL. AS YOU WORK, VERIFY THE QUILT'S DIMENSIONS AFTER EACH PIECED BORDER HAS BEEN ADDED AND, IF NECESSARY, MAKE ADJUSTMENTS TO THE NEXT STRIP BORDER TO BRING THE QUILT INTO COMPLIANCE WITH THE SIZE CALCULATED.

Because this quilt plan ends with a pieced border, it would be easy to increase the size of the quilt by adding one more strip border. For example, if you add a 6" border to the quilt plan, the finished size of the quilt will be 80" x 80". Purchase another 2½ yards of theme fabric if you want to add this border. For this larger quilt, you will need 7½ yards of backing fabric (three panels 29" x 84").

Fabric Requirements

FABRIC	YARDS
1 theme (strip borders, binding)	4½
lt. & med. mixers	3 total, assorted
med. & dk. mixers	3 total, assorted
Backing	4½
Batting	74" x 74"

Reserve the theme fabric needed for all strip borders before cutting patches.

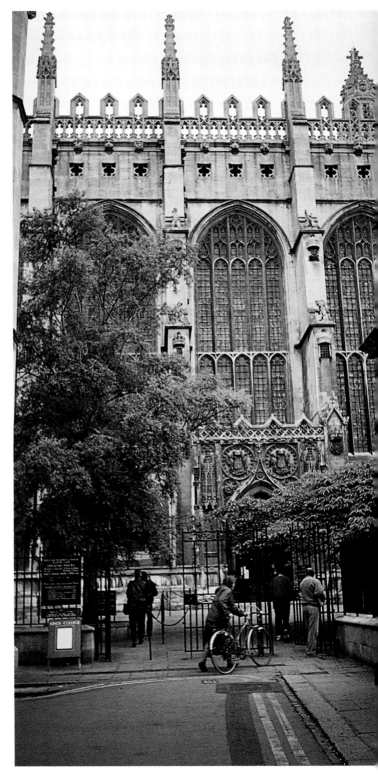

KINGS COLLEGE – CAMBRIDGE UNIVERSITY, CAMBRIDGE

Muggleswick

CENTER BLOCK

The center block is *broderie perse* with elements cut from the theme fabric. You can substitute any 18" (18½" with seam allowances) appliquéd or pieced block that you like.

BORDER ASSEMBLY

Referring to the quilt assembly diagram (page 31) and the cutting instructions for each border, add the following seven borders in sequence.

BORDER 1. SAWTOOTH

Follow the instructions on page 14 to make 36 Sawtooth units, except you will be starting with 3⅛" squares. The units will measure 2¾" with seam allowances.

THEME
18 A   3⅛" x 3⅛", cut once diagonally to make 36 half-square triangles

LT. & MED. MIXERS
18 A   3⅛" x 3⅛", cut once diagonally to make 36 half-square triangles

Border 1 adds 4½" and the quilt measures 23" square.

BORDER 2. STRIP

THEME
2 strips 3" x 23"
2 strips 3" x 28"

Border 2 adds 5" and the quilt measures 28" square.

BORDER 3. FLYING GEESE

Follow the instructions on page 17 to make 40 Flying Geese, 3¼" x 6" with seam allowances.

THEME
20 B   6½" x 6½"
4 D   6" x 6" (corner squares)

LT. & MED. MIXERS
80 C   3½" x 3½"

Border 3 adds 11" and the quilt measures 39" square.

BORDER 4. STRIP

THEME
2 strips 2¼" x 39"
2 strips 2¼" x 42½"

Border 4 adds 3½" and the quilt measures 42½" square.

Muggleswick

QUILT ASSEMBLY

Muggleswick

BORDER 5. FRAMED SQUARE

Follow the instructions on page 16 to make 60 Framed Squares in the 3" size (3½" with seam allowances.)

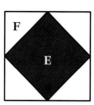

MED. & DK. MIXERS

60 E   3½" x 3½"

LT. & MED. MIXERS

240 F   2" x 2"

Border 5 adds 6" and the quilt measures 48½" square.

BORDER 6. STRIP

THEME

2 strips 2" x 48½"
2 strips 2" x 51½"

Border 6 adds 3" and the quilt measures 51½" square.

BORDER 7. UNEVEN NINE-PATCH

Follow the instructions on page 18 to make 28 Uneven Nine-Patches. They are 6" finished (6½" with seam allowances).

LT. & MED. MIXERS

28 G   3½" x 3½"
112 I   2" x 2"

MED. & DK. MIXERS

112 H   2" x 3½"

THEME

12 J   9¾" x 9¾", cut twice diagonally to make 48 side triangles

8 K   5⅛" x 5⅛", cut once diagonally to make 16 corner triangles

Border 7 adds 17" and the quilt measures 68½" square.

The Uneven Nine-Patches are set on point. Paying close attention to the positioning of setting triangles J and K, sew triangles to opposite sides of each Uneven Nine-Patch to make a diagonal row.

Sew the rows together and add the remaining corner triangles to complete each border section.

Sew the side borders to the quilt, followed by the top and bottom borders.

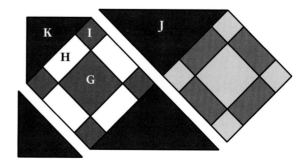

Muggleswick

BORDER 8. (OPTIONAL)

From the extra 2½ yards of theme fabric, cut four 6½" strips parallel to the selvages. Sew the border strips to the quilt and miter the corners.

If Border 8 is added, your quilt should measure 80½" x 80½".

FINISHING

Layer the quilt top, batting, and backing. Baste and quilt the layers. Medallions can be simply and effectively quilted with grid or outline stitching.

Use your favorite technique to bind the layers. The binding yardage is sufficient for any method, including double-fold or bias binding.

PLANNING CHART

Use the construction and planning chart on page 92 to substitute same-sized units or to add borders to your quilt. See Planning Your Own Quilts on page 86 for detailed information on determining the number of units to use in a border and the width of spacer strips.

LOOKING DOWN THE STREET IN BATH, ENGLAND

Pilgrim's Hatch

Pilgrim's Hatch (55¼" x 55¼"), by the author; machine quilted by Kim Diamond

EACH BORDER TREATMENT DEPENDS ON THE ACCURATE CUTTING AND PIECING OF THE PRECEDING BORDERS. USING ¼" SEAM ALLOWANCES IS CRITICAL. AS YOU WORK, VERIFY THE QUILT'S DIMENSIONS AFTER EACH PIECED BORDER HAS BEEN ADDED AND, IF NECESSARY, MAKE ADJUSTMENTS TO THE NEXT STRIP BORDER TO BRING THE QUILT INTO COMPLIANCE WITH THE SIZE CALCULATED.

Fabric Requirements

FABRIC	YARDS
Med. mixer (strip border 1)	¼
1 theme (strip borders 3, 5, and 7)	3
4 mixers	¾ ea.
2 lt. backgrounds	1 ea.
Backing	4
Binding	¾
Batting	60" x 60"

Reserve the theme fabric needed for all strip borders before cutting patches.

TUNBRIDGE WELLS, KENT

Pilgrim's Hatch

QUILT CENTER

A 12" (12½" with seam allowances) Jack in the Pulpit block turned on point forms the center of this medallion quilt. You can substitute any 12" block of your choice.

For rotary cutting, the Jack in the Pulpit block was redrafted with a sightly wider C patch. Patches A, B, and D were resized accordingly. The classic 12" block, with templates, can be found in the book *Carrie Hall Blocks* (AQS, 1999) by the author.

Referring to the block diagram and using the following cutting instructions, make the Jack in the Pulpit block on point. The center with setting triangles is 17" (17½" with seam allowances).

THEME
2 F   9⅜" x 9⅜", cut once diagonally to make 4 half-square triangles

MIXERS
1 A   4⅜" x 4⅜"
4 C   2" x 6"
4 D   2" x 2"
2 E   3⅞" x 3⅞", cut once diagonally to make 4 half-square triangles

BACKGROUND
2 B   3⅝" x 3⅝", cut once diagonally to make 4 half-square triangles
6 E   3⅞" x 3⅞", cut once diagonally to make 12 half-square triangles

BORDER ASSEMBLY

Referring to the quilt assembly diagram (page 37) and the cutting instructions for each border, add the following seven borders in sequence.

BORDER 1. STRIP
MED. MIXER
2 strips 1" x 17½"
2 strips 1" x 18½"

Border 1 adds 1" and the quilt measures 18½" square.

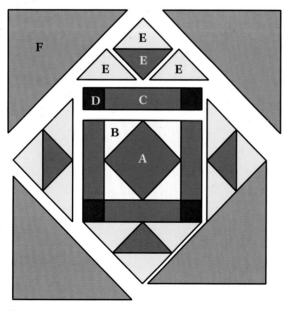

BLOCK ASSEMBLY

Pilgrim's Hatch

QUILT ASSEMBLY. CORNER-TURNING UNITS ARE OUTLINED IN BLACK.

Pilgrim's Hatch

BORDER 2. FRAMED SQUARE

Follow the instructions on page 16 to make 28 Framed Squares in the 3" size (3½" with seam allowances).

MIXERS
28 G 3½" x 3½"

LT. BACKGROUND #1
56 H   2" x 2"

LT. BACKGROUND #2
56 H   2" x 2"

Border 2 adds 6" and the quilt measures 24½" square.

BORDER 3. STRIP

THEME
2 strips 3" x 24½"
2 strips 3" x 29½"

Border 3 adds 5" and the quilt measures 29½" square.

BORDER 4. SAWTOOTH

Refer to page 14 to make 48 Sawtooth units in the 2⅝" finished size (3⅛" with seam allowances).

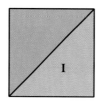

MIXERS
48 I   3½" x 3½", cut once
        diagonally to make 96
        half-square triangles

Border 4 adds 5¼" and the quilt measures 34¾" square.

BORDER 5. STRIP

THEME
2 strips 2½" x 34¾"
2 strips 2½" x 38¾"

Border 5 adds 4" and the quilt measures 38¾" square.

BORDER 6. TRIPLE SQUARE

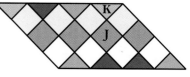

Follow the instructions on pages 11–13 to make 72 Triple Square units with 4 corner-turning units.

CORNER-TURNING UNIT

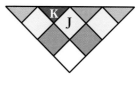

THEME
80 J   2" x 2"

LT. BACKGROUND #1
76 J   2" x 2"

LT. BACKGROUND #2
84 J   2" x 2"

MIXERS
40 K   3½" x 3½", cut twice
        diagonally to make 160
        quarter-square triangles

Border 6 adds 8½" and the quilt measures 47¼" square.

Pilgrim's Hatch

BORDER 7. STRIP

THEME

2 strips 4¾" x 47¼"
2 strips 4¾" x 55¾"

Border 7 adds 8½" and the quilt measures 55¾" square.

FINISHING

Layer the quilt top, batting, and backing. Baste and quilt the layers. Medallions can be simply and effectively quilted with grid or outline stitching.

Use your favorite technique to bind the layers. The binding yardage is sufficient for any method, including double-fold or bias binding.

PLANNING CHART

Use the construction and planning chart on page 93 to substitute same-sized units or to add borders to your quilt. See Planning Your Own Quilts on page 86 for detailed information on determining the number of units to use in a border and the width of spacer strips.

PERIOD ACTORS AT THE OUTDOOR PAVILLION IN TUNBRIDGE WELLS

Scarborough Faire

Scarborough Faire (70" x 77"), by the author; machine quilted by Kim Diamond

EACH BORDER TREATMENT DEPENDS ON THE ACCURATE CUTTING AND PIECING OF THE PRECEDING BORDERS. USING ¼" SEAM ALLOWANCES IS CRITICAL. AS YOU WORK, VERIFY THE QUILT'S DIMENSIONS AFTER EACH PIECED BORDER HAS BEEN ADDED AND, IF NECESSARY, MAKE ADJUSTMENTS TO THE NEXT STRIP BORDER TO BRING THE QUILT INTO COMPLIANCE WITH THE SIZE CALCULATED.

Notice that this quilt is rectangular, which is accomplished in Border 8 by adding one kind of border to the top and bottom of the quilt and a different border treatment on the sides.

Fabric Requirements

FABRIC	YARDS
1 theme (strip borders 3, 7, and 9)	3½
2 lt. mixers	1 ea.
Dk. mixer #1	½
Dk. mixer #2 (strip border 1)	½
Dk. mixer #3 (strip border 5)	½
6 med. mixers	¾ ea.
Backing	5
Binding	¾
Batting	78" x 84"

Reserve the theme fabric needed for all strip borders before cutting patches.

FLOWER STAND IN FRONT OF AN OLD CHURCH IN SOUTH KENSINGTON

Scarborough Faire

CENTER BLOCK

Referring to the block diagram and using the following cutting instructions, make the Feathered Star block. You can substitute any 19½" (20" with seam allowances) appliquéd or pieced block that you like.

Use the patterns on pages 46–49 for cutting your pieces.

FEATHERED STAR
THEME
  64 F
    4 G
    4 H

LT. MIXER
  1 A

DK. MIXER #1
  8 B
  8 D

DK. MIXER #2
  8 E
 48 F

DK. MIXER #3
  8 C

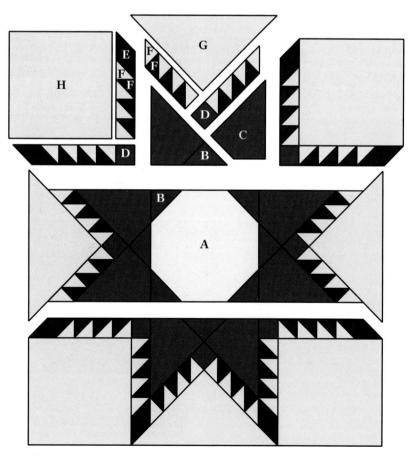

BLOCK ASSEMBLY

Scarborough Faire

QUILT ASSEMBLY. CORNER-TURNING UNITS ARE OUTLINED IN ORANGE.

Scarborough Faire

BORDER ASSEMBLY

Referring to the quilt assembly diagram (page 43) and the cutting instructions for each border, add the following nine borders in sequence.

BORDER 1. STRIP

DK. MIXER #2

4 strips 2" x 20"

THEME

4   I   2" x 2" (corner squares)

Border 1 adds 3" and the quilt measures 23" square.

BORDER 2. HOUR GLASS

Follow the instructions on page 15 to make 44 Hour Glass units in the 2¼" size (2¾" with seam allowances).

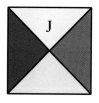

ASSORTED COLORS

44 J   3½" x 3½", cut twice diagonally to make 176 quarter-square triangles

Border 2 adds 4½" and the quilt measures 27½" square.

BORDER 3. STRIP

THEME

4 strips 3½" x 27½"

DK. MIXER #2

4   K   3½" x 3½" (corner squares)

Border 3 adds 6" and the quilt measures 33½" square.

BORDER 4. FRAMED SQUARE

Follow the instructions on page 16 to make 48 Framed Squares in the 3" size (3½" with seam allowances).

ASSORTED COLORS

48 L   3½" x 3½"
192 M   2" x 2"

Border 4 adds 6" and the quilt measures 39½" square.

BORDER 5. STRIP

DK. MIXER #1

4 strips 2¼" x 39½"

DK. MIXER #3

4   N   2¼" x 2¼" (corner squares)

Border 5 adds 3½" and the quilt measures 43" square.

Scarborough Faire

BORDER 6. TRIPLE SQUARE

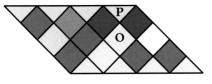

Follow the instructions on pages 11–13 to make 80 Triple-Square units and 4 corner-turning units.

CORNER-TURNING UNIT

ASSORTED COLORS

264 O	2" x 2"	
44 P	3½" x 3½", cut twice diagonally to make 176 quarter-square triangles	

Border 6 adds 8½" and the quilt measures 51½" square.

BORDER 7. STRIP

THEME
4 strips 2½" x 51½"

LT. & MED. MIXERS
4 Q   2⅞" x 2⅞", cut once diagonally to make 8 half-square triangles

Pair light and medium triangles and sew them together to make 4 Sawtooth corner squares.

Border 7 adds 4" and the quilt measures 55½" square.

BORDER 8. FLYING GEESE

Follow the instructions on page 17 to make 40 Flying Geese in the 2¾" x 5½" size (3¼" x 6" with seam allowances).

ASSORTED COLORS

20 R	6½" x 6½"	
80 S	3½" x 3½"	

Make 2 border strips of 20 Flying Geese, flying in opposite directions, and sew them to the top and bottom of the quilt.

The Flying Geese units add 11" and the quilt measures 55½" x 66½".

SAWTOOTH UNITS

Follow the instructions on page 14 to make 66 Sawtooth units, except you will be starting with 2⅞" squares. The finished squares will be 2" (2½" with seam allowances).

Scarborough Faire

ASSORTED COLORS

33 T 2⅞" x 2⅞", cut once
diagonally to make 66
half-square triangles

The Sawtooth units add 4" and the quilt measures 59½" x 66½".

BORDER 9.
STRIP (MITERED CORNERS)
THEME

2 strips 6" x 77¾"
2 strips 6" x 70¾"

Border 9 adds 11" and the quilt measures 70½" x 77½".

FINISHING

Layer the quilt top, batting, and backing. Baste and quilt the layers. Medallions can be simply and effectively quilted with grid or outline stitching.

Use your favorite technique to bind the layers. The binding yardage is sufficient for any method, including double-fold or bias binding.

PLANNING CHART

Use the construction and planning chart on page 101 to substitute same-sized units or to add borders to your quilt. See Planning Your Own Quilts on page 86 for detailed information on determining the number of units to use in a border and the width of spacer strips.

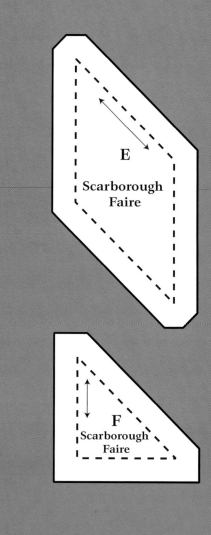

Scarborough Faire

REFER TO THE BLOCK ASSEMBLY DIAGRAM ON PAGE 42.

A

Scarborough Faire

Scarborough Faire

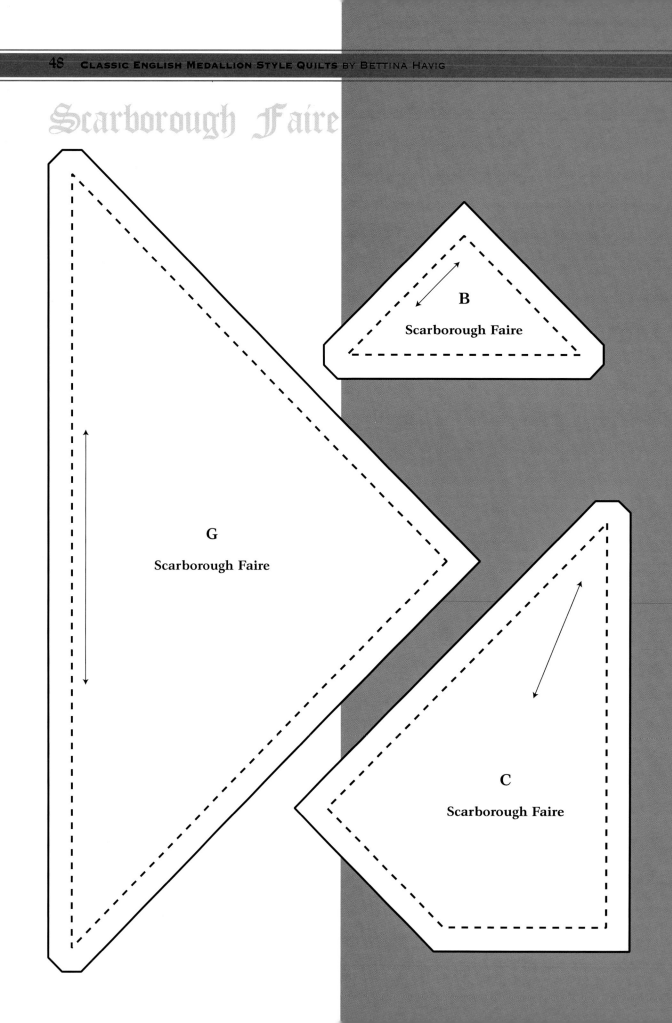

B

Scarborough Faire

G

Scarborough Faire

C

Scarborough Faire

Scarborough Faire

REFER TO THE BLOCK ASSEMBLY DIAGRAM ON PAGE 42.

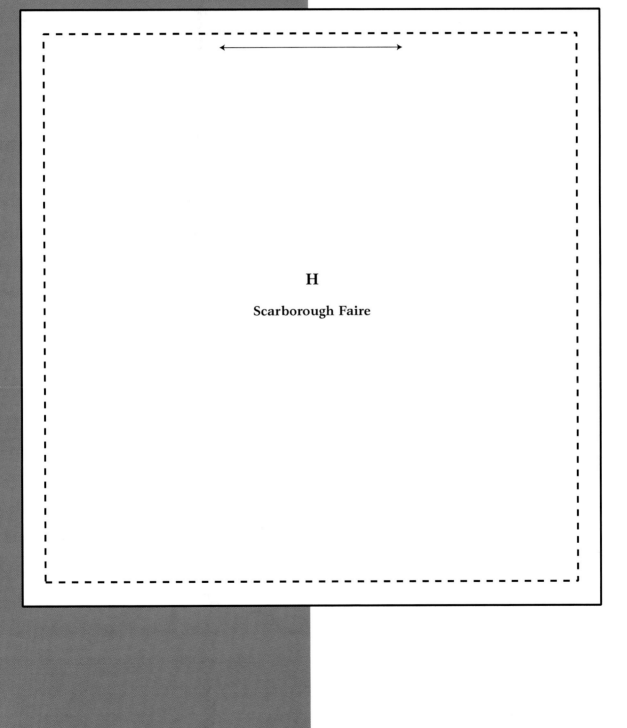

H

Scarborough Faire

Barnard Castle

Barnard Castle (73" x 73"), by the author; machine quilted by Kim Diamond

EACH BORDER TREATMENT DEPENDS ON THE ACCURATE CUTTING AND PIECING OF THE PRECEDING BORDERS. USING ¼" SEAM ALLOWANCES IS CRITICAL. AS YOU WORK, VERIFY THE QUILT'S DIMENSIONS AFTER EACH PIECED BORDER HAS BEEN ADDED AND, IF NECESSARY, MAKE ADJUSTMENTS TO THE NEXT STRIP BORDER TO BRING THE QUILT INTO COMPLIANCE WITH THE SIZE CALCULATED.

Fabric Requirements

FABRIC	YARDS
1 theme*	4¾
1 bright accent	½
Background 1	¾
Background 2	½
1 med. or dk. mixer	¼
6 or more med. mixers	¾ ea.
Stripe (optional)	2½
Backing	4¾
Binding	¾
Batting	80" x 80"

* The theme fabric yardage includes all strip borders. If using the optional striped fabric for Borders 5 and 7, you can reduce the theme fabric to 3 yards.

Reserve the theme fabric needed for all strip borders before cutting patches.

RUINS OF LUDLOW CASTLE, BUILT IN THE LATE ELEVENTH CENTURY

Barnard Castle

QUILT CENTER

The center of the medallion contains a Mariner's Compass block. You can substitute any 19¾" (20¼" with seam allowances) block of your choice.

Referring to the block diagram and using the following cutting instructions, make the Mariner's Compass block.

Use the patch patterns on pages 56–57 for cutting your pieces.

THEME OR STRIPE
8 A

DARK MIXER
8 B

BRIGHT ACCENT
8 C

MEDIUM MIXER
16 D

BACKGROUND
32 E
4 F

To complete the center medallion, turn the Compass block on point, and cut two 14⅞" squares from the theme fabric. Cut the squares in half diagonally to yield 4 half-square triangles (G patches, page 53) to frame the Compass block.

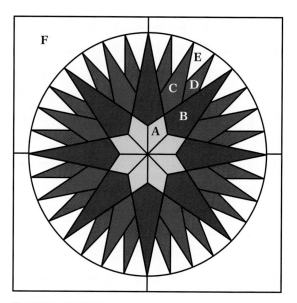

BLOCK ASSEMBLY

BORDER ASSEMBLY

Referring to the quilt assembly diagram (page 53) and the cutting instructions for each border, add the following seven borders in sequence.

BORDER 1. STRIP
BRIGHT ACCENT
2 strips 2¼" x 28½"
2 strips 2¼" x 32"

Border 1 adds 3½" and the quilt measures 32" square.

Barnard Castle

QUILT ASSEMBLY

Barnard Castle

BORDER 2. DOGTOOTH

Follow the instructions on page 14 to make 52 Dogtooth triangles.

DARK MIXERS

6 H   6½" x 6½", cut twice diagonally to make 24 quarter-square triangles

BACKGROUND

7 H   6½" x 6½", cut twice diagonally to make 28 quarter-square triangles

Sew the triangles together in 4 strips with 6 inside and 7 outside triangles. Sew the rows to the quilt and connect the seams at the corners.

Border 2 adds 5¼" and the quilt measures 37¼" square.

BORDER 3. STRIP

THEME

2 strips 3⅛" x 37¼"
2 strips 3⅛" x 42½"

Border 3 adds 5¼" and the quilt measures 42½" square.

BORDER 4. FRAMED SQUARE

Follow the instructions on page 16 to make 32 Framed Squares in the 6" size (6½" with seam allowances).

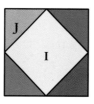

THEME

32 I   6½" x 6½"

ASSORTED MIXERS

128 J   3½" x 3½"

Border 4 adds 12" and the quilt measures 54½" square.

BORDER 5.

STRIP (MITERED CORNERS)

THEME OR STRIPE

4 strips 6⅛" x 66"

Border 5 adds 11¼" and the quilt measures 65¾" square.

BORDER 6. SAWTOOTH

Follow the instructions on page 14 to make 120 Sawtooth units, except you will be starting with 3⅛" squares. The units will measure 2¾" with seam allowances.

ASSORTED COLORS

60 K   3⅛" x 3⅛", cut once diagonally to make 120 half-square triangles

THEME

60 K   3⅛" x 3⅛", cut once diagonally to make 120 half-square triangles

Barnard Castle

Border 6 adds 4½" and the quilt measures 70¼" square.

BORDER 7. STRIP

THEME OR STRIPE

    4 strips 2⅛" x 70¼"

    4 L   2⅛" x 2⅛" (corner squares)

Border 7 adds 3¼" and the quilt measures 73½" square.

FINISHING

Layer the quilt top, batting, and backing. Baste and quilt the layers. Medallions can be simply and effectively quilted with grid or outline stitching.

Use your favorite technique to bind the layers. The binding yardage is sufficient for any method, including double-fold or bias binding.

PLANNING CHART

Use the construction and planning chart on page 90 to substitute same-sized units or to add borders to your quilt. See Planning Your Own Quilts on page 86 for detailed information on determining the number of units to use in a border and the width of spacer strips.

ABOVE: CRAFT FAIRE AT LUDLOW CASTLE GROUNDS

RIGHT: INTERIOR RUINS AT LUDLOW CASTLE

Barnard Castle

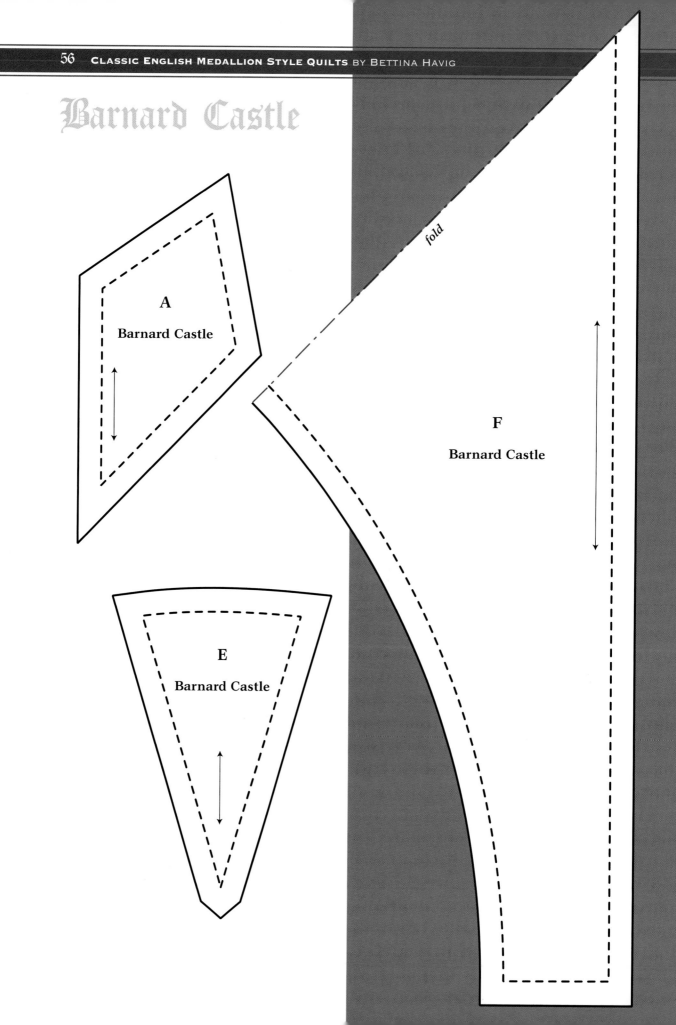

A
Barnard Castle

fold

F
Barnard Castle

E
Barnard Castle

Barnard Castle

REFER TO THE BLOCK ASSEMBLY
DIAGRAM ON PAGE 52.

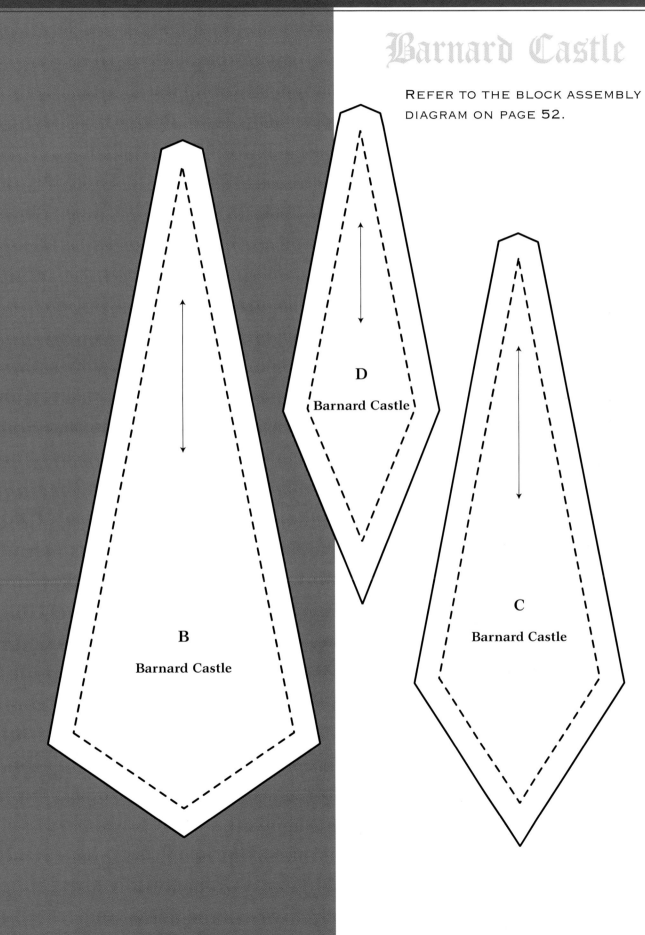

D
Barnard Castle

C
Barnard Castle

B
Barnard Castle

Little Snoring (51" x 57"), by the author; machine quilted by Kim Diamond

EACH BORDER TREATMENT DEPENDS ON THE ACCURATE CUTTING AND PIECING OF THE PRECEDING BORDERS. USING ¼" SEAM ALLOWANCES IS CRITICAL. AS YOU WORK, VERIFY THE QUILT'S DIMENSIONS AFTER EACH PIECED BORDER HAS BEEN ADDED AND, IF NECESSARY, MAKE ADJUSTMENTS TO THE NEXT STRIP BORDER TO BRING THE QUILT INTO COMPLIANCE WITH THE SIZE CALCULATED.

Fabric Requirements

FABRIC	YARDS
1 theme	2
2 lt. mixers	1 ea.
5 med. or dk. mixers	½ ea.
2 bright mixers	½ ea.
Backing	3¾
Binding	¾
Batting	56" x 62"

Reserve the theme fabric needed for all strip borders before cutting patches.

ENCLOSED GARDEN AT KENSINGTON PALACE, SOUTH KENSINGTON, LONDON

Little Snoring

QUILT CENTER

The center of the medallion is a Joseph's Coat block. You can substitute any 15" (15½" with seam allowances) block of your choice.

Referring to the block diagram and using the following cutting instructions, make the Joseph's Coat block.

THEME

    1 A   4¾" x 4¾"

LT. MIXER #1

    32 B   Use pattern on page 63.

DK. MIXER

    4 C   3⅞" x 3⅞", cut once diagonally to make 8 half-square triangles

BRIGHT MIXERS

    4 B   Use pattern on page 63.
    4 D   2⅝" x 2⅝"
    4 E   3½" x 3½"

MED. MIXERS

    4 C   3⅞" x 3⅞", cut once diagonally to make 8 half-square triangles

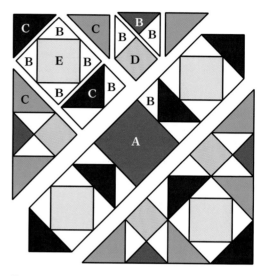

BLOCK ASSEMBLY

BORDER ASSEMBLY

Referring to the quilt assembly diagram (page 61) and the cutting instructions for each border, add the following five borders in sequence.

BORDER 1. STRIP

LT. MIXER #2

    2 strips 2" x 15½"
    2 strips 2" x 18½"

Border 1 adds 3" and the quilt measures 18½" square.

Little Snoring

QUILT ASSEMBLY

Little Snoring

BORDER 2. FRAMED SQUARE

Refer to page 16 to make 28 Framed Squares in the 3" size (3½" with seam allowances).

BRIGHT MIXER #1
14 F   3½" x 3½"

BRIGHT MIXER #2
14 F   3½" x 3½"

THEME
56 G   2" x 2"

MIXERS
56 G   2" x 2"

Border 2 adds 6" and the quilt measures 24½" square.

BORDER 3.
STRIP AND FLYING GEESE
BRIGHT MIXERS
2 strips   3½" x 24½"
2 strips   2½" x 30½"
2 strips   2" x 30½"
24 H   3½" x 3½"

THEME
96 I   2" x 2"

Sew a 3½" strip to each side of the quilt and a 2½" strip to the top and bottom.

Follow the directions on page 17 to make 48 Flying Geese (patches H and I) in the 1¼" x 2½" size (1¾" x 3" with seam allowances).

See the quilt photo for placement, and sew the Flying Geese into 2 rows of 24 units each. Reverse the direction of the geese at the middle of each row. Sew a Flying Geese row to the top and bottom of the quilt.

Add the 2" strip border to the top and bottom of the quilt.

Border 3 adds 6" to the width and 12" to the length, and the quilt measures 30½" x 36½".

BORDER 4. UNEVEN NINE-PATCH

Follow the instructions on page 18 to make 26 Uneven Nine-Patches that are 6" square (6½" with seam allowances).

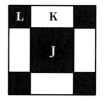

DK. & BRIGHT MIXERS
26 J   3½" x 3½"
104 L   2" x 2"

BRIGHT MIXER #1
52 K   2" x 3½"

BRIGHT MIXER #2
52 K   2" x 3½"

Border 4 adds 12" and the quilt measures 42½" x 48½".

$\mathfrak{Little\ Snoring}$

BORDER 5. STRIP
THEME #2

2 strips 5" x 48½"
2 strips 5" x 51½"

Border 5 adds 9" and the quilt measures 51½" x 57½".

FINISHING

Layer the quilt top, batting, and backing. Baste and quilt the layers. Medallions can be simply and effectively quilted with grid or outline stitching.

Use your favorite technique to bind the layers. The binding yardage is sufficient for any method, including double-fold or bias binding.

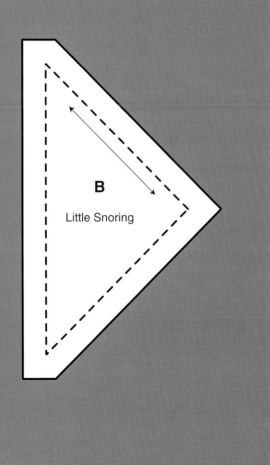

B
Little Snoring

PLANNING CHART

Use the construction and planning chart on page 91 to substitute same-sized units or to add borders to your quilt. See Planning Your Own Quilts on page 86 for detailed information on determining the number of units to use in a border and the width of spacer strips.

KENSINGTON PALACE GATES. THE PALACE WAS HOME TO QUEEN ANNE, QUEEN VICTORIA, AND PRINCESS DIANA, AMONG OTHERS.

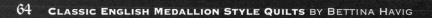

Rainbow Hill

Rainbow Hill (72" x 72"), by the author; machine quilted by Kim Diamond

EACH BORDER TREATMENT DEPENDS ON THE ACCURATE CUTTING AND PIECING OF THE PRECEDING BORDERS. USING $\frac{1}{4}$" SEAM ALLOWANCES IS CRITICAL. AS YOU WORK, VERIFY THE QUILT'S DIMENSIONS AFTER EACH PIECED BORDER HAS BEEN ADDED AND, IF NECESSARY, MAKE ADJUSTMENTS TO THE NEXT STRIP BORDER TO BRING THE QUILT INTO COMPLIANCE WITH THE SIZE CALCULATED.

Fabric Requirements

FABRIC	YARDS
1 theme	4
8 or more mixers	¾ ea.
2 lt. backgrounds	1½ ea.
Backing and binding	5¼
Batting	78" x 78"

Reserve the theme fabric needed for all strip borders before cutting patches.

PAY-TO-USE PUBLIC PARK IN BATH

Rainbow Hill

CENTER BLOCK

The center of the medallion is a Lucinda's Star block. You can substitute any 18" (18½" with seam allowances) block of your choice.

Refer to the block diagram and use the following cutting instructions and the patterns on pages 70–71 to make the Lucinda's Star block.

THEME
    8 A
    8 C

BACKGROUND
    40 B
    4 D

ASSORTED (INCLUDE SOME THEME)
    56 B

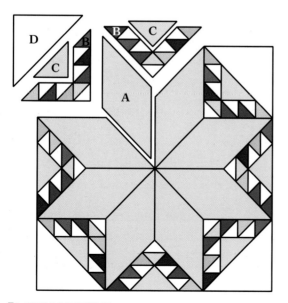

BLOCK ASSEMBLY

BORDER ASSEMBLY

Referring to the quilt assembly diagram (page 67) and the cutting instructions for each border, add the following eight borders in sequence.

BORDER 1. SAWTOOTH

Follow the instructions on page 14 to make 40 Sawtooth units, except you will be starting with 2⅞" squares. The units will measure 2½" with seam allowances.

ASSORTED (INCLUDE SOME THEME)
    40 E   2⅞" x 2⅞", cut once
            diagonally to make 80
            half-square triangles

Border 1 adds 4" and the quilt measures 22½" square.

BORDER 2. STRIP

THEME
    4 strips 3" x 22½"

BACKGROUND #1
    4 F   3" x 3" (corner squares)

Border 2 adds 5" and the quilt measures 27½" square.

Rainbow Hill

QUILT ASSEMBLY. CORNER-TURNING UNITS ARE OUTLINED IN BLACK.

Rainbow Hill

BORDER 3. HOUR GLASS

Refer to page 15 to make 52 Hour Glass units in the 2¼" size (2¾" with seam allowances).

ASSORTED (INCLUDE SOME THEME)

52 G	3½" x 3½", cut twice diagonally to make 208 quarter-square triangles	

Border 3 adds 4½" and the quilt measures 32" square.

BORDER 4. BAR

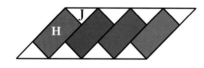

Refer to page 11 to make 60 Bar units and 4 corner-turning units.

CORNER-TURNING UNIT

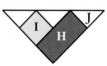

ASSORTED COLORS

64 H	2" x 3½"	
4 I	2" x 2"	

BACKGROUND

33 J	3½" x 3½", cut twice diagonally to make 132 quarter-square triangles	

Border 4 adds 6¼" and the quilt measures 38¼" square.

BORDER 5. STRIP (MITERED CORNERS)

THEME

4 strips 2⅝" x 42¾"

Border 5 adds 4¼" and the quilt measures 42½" square.

BORDER 6. FRAMED SQUARE

Refer to page 16 to make 60 Framed Squares in the 3" size (3½" with seam allowances).

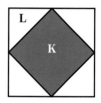

ASSORTED

60 K	3½" x 3½"	

BACKGROUND

240 L	2" x 2"	

Border 6 adds 6" and the quilt measures 48½" square.

BORDER 7. FRAMED SQUARE

Refer to page 16 to make 36 Framed Squares in the 6" size (6½" with seam allowances).

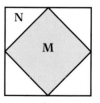

ASSORTED (INCLUDE SOME THEME)

36 M	6½" x 6½"	

BACKGROUND

144 N	3½" x 3½"	

Border 7 adds 12" and the quilt measures 60½" square.

Rainbow Hill

BORDER 8. STRIP (MITERED CORNERS)

THEME

4 strips 6½" x 72¾"

Border 8 adds 12" and the quilt measures 72½" square.

FINISHING

Layer the quilt top, batting, and backing. Baste and quilt the layers. Medallions can be simply and effectively quilted with grid or outline stitching.

Use your favorite technique to bind the layers. The binding yardage is sufficient for any method, including double-fold or bias binding.

PLANNING CHART

Use the construction and planning chart on page 96 to substitute same-sized units or to add borders to your quilt. See Planning Your Own Quilts on page 86 for detailed information on determining the number of units to use in a border and the width of spacer strips.

CITY OF BATH VIEWED FROM A DISTANCE

PAY-TO-USE PUBLIC PARK IN BATH

Rainbow Hill

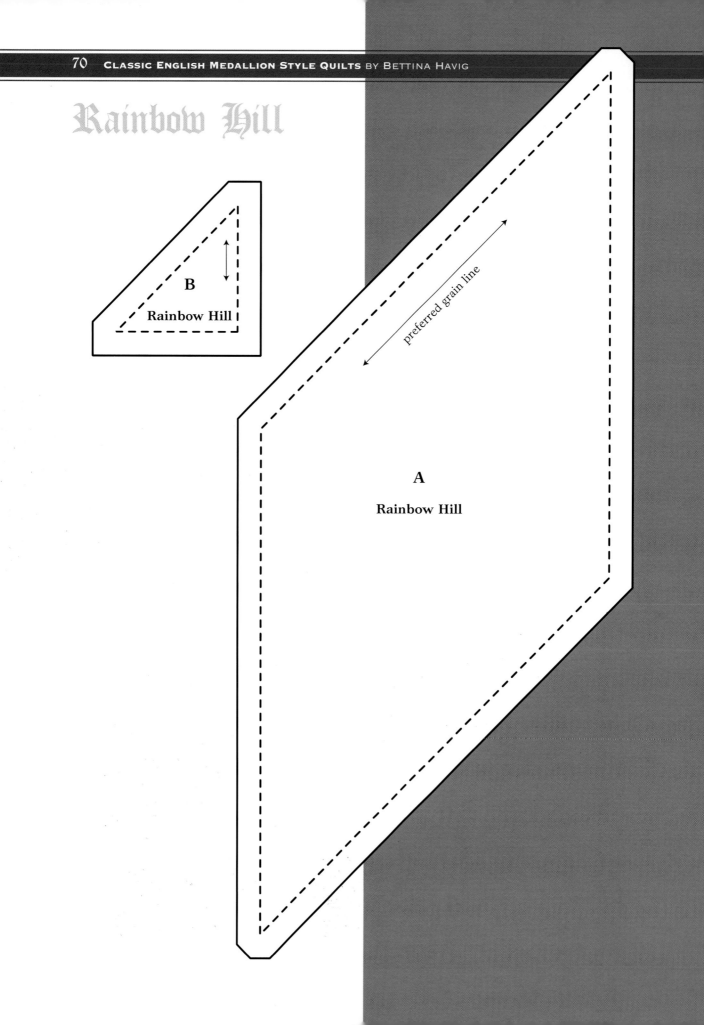

B

Rainbow Hill

preferred grain line

A

Rainbow Hill

Rainbow Hill

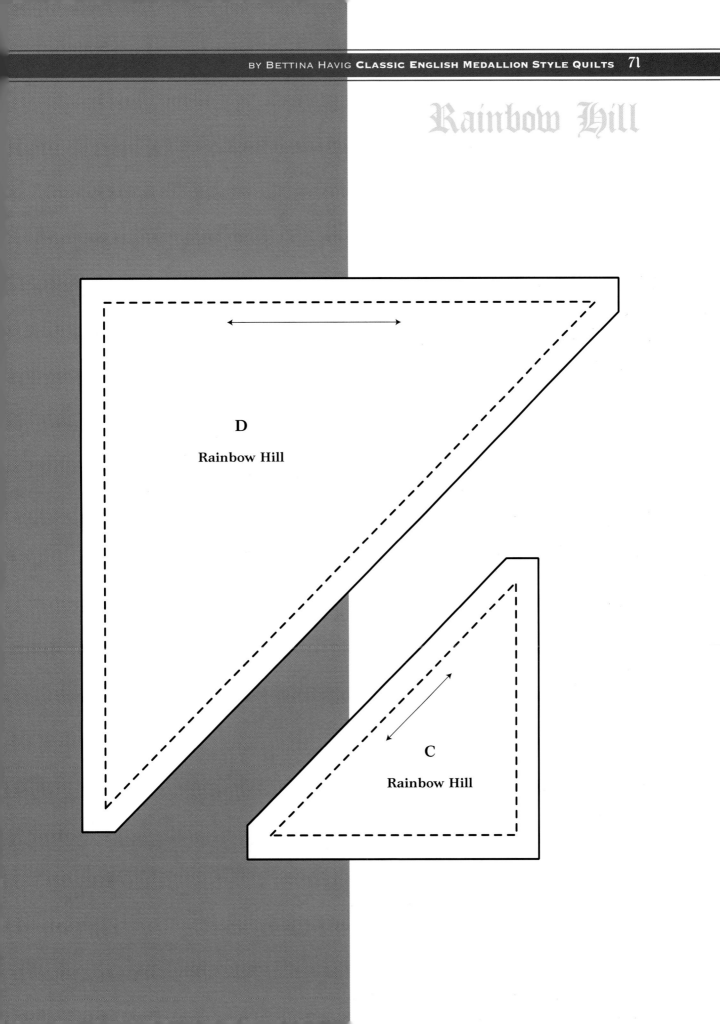

D

Rainbow Hill

C

Rainbow Hill

Rest & Be Thankful

Rest & Be Thankful (75" x 75"), by the author; machine quilted by Kim Diamond

EACH BORDER TREATMENT DEPENDS ON THE ACCURATE CUTTING AND PIECING OF THE PRECEDING BORDERS. USING ¼" SEAM ALLOWANCES IS CRITICAL. AS YOU WORK, VERIFY THE QUILT'S DIMENSIONS AFTER EACH PIECED BORDER HAS BEEN ADDED AND, IF NECESSARY, MAKE ADJUSTMENTS TO THE NEXT STRIP BORDER TO BRING THE QUILT INTO COMPLIANCE WITH THE SIZE CALCULATED.

Note that this quilt has two theme fabrics, one light and one medium-dark print.

Fabric Requirements

FABRIC	YARDS
Theme #1 (med.-dk.)	4
Theme #2 (lt.)	2
Lt. mixers	2 total, assorted
Med. & med. dk. mixers	3 total, assorted
Backing	5
Binding	¾
Batting	80" x 80"

Reserve the theme fabric needed for all strip borders before cutting patches.

HIGHGATE CEMETERY, LONDON. STAIRWAY TO INNER-CIRCLE CHAMBERS.

Rest & Be Thankful

QUILT CENTER

The center block is *broderie perse*. The elements of the appliqué are cut from one of the theme fabrics. You can substitute any 18" (18½" with seam allowances) appliquéd or pieced block that you like.

BORDER ASSEMBLY

Referring to the quilt assembly diagram (page 75) and the cutting instructions for each border, add the following 10 borders in sequence.

BORDER 1. FRAMED SQUARE

Follow the instructions on page 16 to make 28 framed squares in the 3" size (3½" with seam allowances).

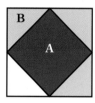

MED. MIXERS
28 A   3½" x 3½"

LT. MIXERS
112 B   2" x 2"

Border 1 adds 6" and the quilt measures 24½" square.

BORDER 2. STRIP
THEME #1
2 strips 2" x 24½"
2 strips 2" x 27½"

Border 2 adds 3" and the quilt measures 27½" square.

BORDER 3. HOUR GLASS

Follow the instructions on page 15 to make 52 Hour Glass units in the 2¼" size (2¾" with seam allowances).

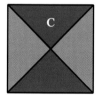

MED. AND LT. MIXERS
52 C   3½" x 3½", cut twice
        diagonally to make 208
        quarter-square triangles

Border 3 adds 4½" and the quilt measures 32" square.

BORDER 4. STRIP
THEME #1
2 strips 3¾" x 32"
2 strips 3¾" x 38½"

Border 4 adds 6½" and the quilt measures 38½" square.

Rest & Be Thankful

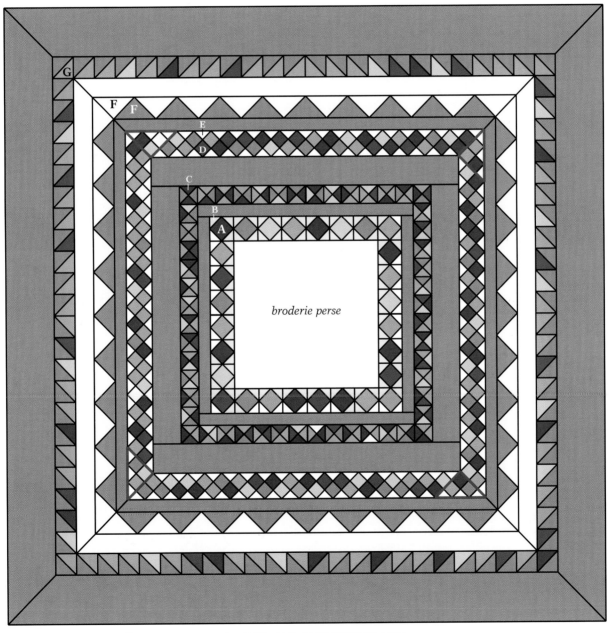

QUILT ASSEMBLY. CORNER-TURNING UNITS ARE OUTLINED IN RED.

Rest & Be Thankful

BORDER 5. DOUBLE SQUARE

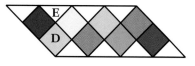

Follow the instructions on page 13 to make 72 Double Squares and 4 corner-turning units.

CORNER-TURNING UNIT

MED. MIXERS
156 D   2" x 2"

LT. MIXERS
39 E   3½" x 3½", cut twice diagonally to make 156 quarter-square triangles

Border 5 adds 6¼" and the quilt measures 44¾" square.

BORDER 6. STRIP (MITERED CORNERS)
THEME #1
4 strips 2" x 48"

Border 6 adds 3" and the quilt measures 47¾" square.

BORDER 7. DOGTOOTH

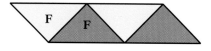

Follow the instructions on page 14 to make 76 Dogtooth triangles in the larger size (2⅝" x 5¼").

THEME #1
9 F   6½" x 6½", cut twice diagonally to make 36 quarter-square triangles

THEME #2
10 F   6½" x 6½", cut twice diagonally to make 40 quarter-square triangles

Border 7 adds 5¼" and the quilt measures 53" square.

BORDER 8. STRIP (MITERED CORNERS)
THEME #2
4 strips 3⅛" x 58½"

Border 8 adds 5¼" and the quilt measures 58¼" square.

BORDER 9. SAWTOOTH
Follow the instructions on page 14 to make 92 Sawtooth units in the 2⅝" size (3⅛" with seam allowances).

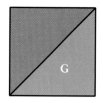

Rest & Be Thankful

ASSORTED COLORS

92 G   3½" x 3½", cut once diagonally to make 184 half-square triangles

Border 9 adds 5¼" and the quilt measures 63½" square.

BORDER 10. STRIP (MITERED CORNERS)
THEME #1

4 strips 6½" x 75¾"

Border 10 adds 12" and the quilt measures 75½" square.

FINISHING

Layer the quilt top, batting, and backing. Baste and quilt the layers. Medallions can be simply and effectively quilted with grid or outline stitching.

Use your favorite technique to bind the layers. The binding yardage is sufficient for any method, including double-fold or bias binding.

PLANNING CHART

Use the construction and planning chart on page 99 to substitute same-sized units or to add borders to your quilt. See Planning Your Own Quilts on page 86 for detailed information on determining the number of units to use in a border and the width of spacer strips.

GATEWAY TO THE EGYPTIAN AVENUE IN HIGHGATE CEMETERY, LONDON

Peacehaven

Peacehaven (80¼" x 90¼"), by the author; machine quilted by Kim Diamond

EACH BORDER TREATMENT DEPENDS ON THE ACCURATE CUTTING AND PIECING OF THE PRECEDING BORDERS. USING ¼" SEAM ALLOWANCES IS CRITICAL. AS YOU WORK, VERIFY THE QUILT'S DIMENSIONS AFTER EACH PIECED BORDER HAS BEEN ADDED AND, IF NECESSARY, MAKE ADJUSTMENTS TO THE NEXT STRIP BORDER TO BRING THE QUILT INTO COMPLIANCE WITH THE SIZE CALCULATED.

Fabric Requirements

FABRIC	YARDS
Theme (strip borders 7 & 9)	4½
Rose (strip borders 1 & 3)	1⅛
Tan (strip border 4)	1¼
4 dk. mixers	1 ea.
2 med. mixers	¾ ea.
Lt. background	1
Backing	7¾
Binding	¾
Batting	90" x 108"

Reserve the theme fabric needed for all strip borders before cutting patches.

WESTMINSTER ABBEY, THE BENEDICTINE ABBEY CHURCH BEGUN BY EDWARD THE CONFESSOR IN 1050.

Peacehaven

CENTER PANEL

At the center of the medallion is a 10" Friendship block turned on point. You may substitute any 10" (finished) block that you choose.

Use the following instructions and the pattern piece on page 85 to make the Friendship block. This traditional block was slightly altered when drafted so that most of the pieces could be rotary cut.

FRIENDSHIP BLOCK

DK. MIXER

    1 A   3½" x 3½"

    2 D   4¼" x 4¼", cut twice diagonally to make 8 quarter-square triangles

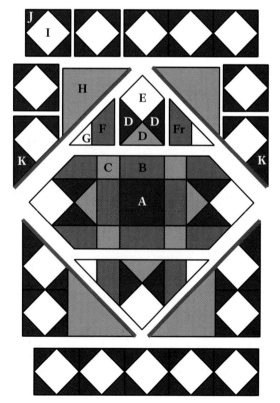

CENTER PANEL. FRIENDSHIP BLOCK OUT-LINED IN RED.

ROSE

    4 B   2" x 3½"

    4 F   Use the pattern on page 85.

    4 Fr   Use the pattern on page 85.

MED. MIXER

    4 C   2" x 2"

    2 D   3" x 3", cut once diagonally to make 4 half-square triangles

THEME

    4 E   2⅝" x 2⅝"

    1 G   3¼" x 3¼", cut twice diagonally to make 4 quarter-square triangles

Add the following pieces to complete the medallion center panel. It should measure 15½" x 21½" with seam allowances.

SETTING TRIANGLE

MED. MIXER

    2 H   5⅜" x 5⅜", cut once diagonally to make 4 half-square triangles

FRAMED SQUARE

Follow the instructions on page 16 to make 14 Framed Squares in the 3" size (3½" with seam allowances). Make 2 each of the partial Framed Squares as shown.

QUILT ASSEMBLY

Peacehaven

THEME

18 I   3½" x 3½"

DK. MIXER

64 J   2" x 2"

1 K   4¼" x 4¼", cut twice
diagonally to make 4
quarter-square triangles

BORDER ASSEMBLY

Referring to the quilt assembly diagram (page 81) and the cutting instructions for each border, add the following nine borders in sequence.

BORDER 1. STRIP

ROSE

2 strips 2" x 15½"
2 strips 2" x 21½"

THEME

4 corner squares 2" x 2"

Border 1 adds 3" and the quilt measures 18½" x 24½".

BORDER 2. UNEVEN NINE-PATCH

Follow the instructions on page 18 to make 18 Uneven Nine-Patches in the 6" size (6½" with seam allowances). For each L fabric, Ms and Ns are cordinated in groups of 4.

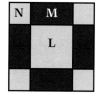

DK. MIXER

7 L   3½" x 3½"
44 M   2" x 3½"
28 N   2" x 2"

MED. MIXER

11 L   3½" x 3½"
28 M   2" x 3½"
44 N   2" x 2"

Border 2 adds 12" and the quilt measures 30½" x 36½".

BORDER 3. STRIP

ROSE

2 strips 2" x 30½"
2 strips 2" x 36½"

TAN

4 corner squares 2" x 2"

Border 3 adds 3" and the quilt measures 33½" x 39½".

BORDER 4. STRIP

TAN

2 strips 1" x 39½"
2 strips 2" x 34½"

Sew the 1" strips to the sides of the quilt, then add the 2" strips to the top and bottom.

Border 4 adds 3" in length and 1" in width and the quilt measures 34½" x 42½".

Peacehaven

BORDER 5. EVENING STAR

Follow the instructions on page 19 to make 18 dark Evening Stars and 8 rose Evening Stars. The units will be 6" (6½" with seam allowances). Reserve 4 of the rose stars for the corners of Border 9.

DK. MIXERS

   18 O   3½" x 3½"

   72 P   2⅜" x 2⅜", cut once diagonally to make 144 half-square triangles (Select fabrics in 4's to coordinate with centers.)

ROSE

   8 O   3½" x 3½"

   32 P   2⅜" x 2⅜", cut once diagonally to make 64 half-square triangles (Select fabrics in 4's to coordinate with centers.)

THEME

   26 Q   4¼" x 4¼", cut twice diagonally to make 104 quarter-square triangles

 104 R   2" x 2"

   9 S   9¾" x 9¾", cut twice diagonally to make 36 quarter-square triangles

   8 T   5⅛" x 5⅛", cut once diagonally to make 16 half-square triangles

Border 5 adds 17" and the quilt measures 51½" x 59½".

BORDER 6. SAWTOOTH

Follow the instructions on page 14 to make the Sawtooth border, except you will start with 5⅛" squares. The units will measure 4¾" with seam allowances. When joining border 6 to border 5, notice that there are 2 Sawteeth for every Evening Star.

DK. MIXERS

   28 U   5⅛" x 5⅛", cut once diagonally to make 56 half-square triangles

LT. BACKGROUND

   28 U   5⅛" x 5⅛", cut once diagonally to make 56 half-square triangles

Border 6 adds 8½" and the quilt measures 60" x 68".

Peacehaven

BORDER 7. STRIP

THEME

> 2 strips 3¼" x 60"
>
> 2 strips 2¼" x 73½"

Sew the 3¼" strips to the top and bottom, then add the 2¼" strips to the sides of the quilt.

Border 7 adds 5½" to the length and 3½" to the width and the quilt measures 63½" x 73½".

BORDER 8. DOGTOOTH

Follow the instructions on page 14 to make the larger Dogtooth triangles.

DK. MIXERS

> 13 V 6½" x 6½", cut twice diagonally to make 52 quarter-square triangles
>
> 2 W 3½" x 3½", cut once diagonally to make 4 half-square triangles

MED. MIXERS

> 12 V 6½" x 6½", cut twice diagonally to make 48 quarter-square triangles
>
> 6 W 3½" x 3½", cut once diagonally to make 12 half-square triangles

Refer to the Quilt Assembly diagram, page 81, for the placement of the corner patches.

Border 8 adds 5¼" and the quilt measures 68¾" x 78¾".

BORDER 9. STRIP

THEME

> 2 strips 6½" x 68¾"
>
> 2 strips 6½" x 78¾"

Add the 4 remaining rose Evening Stars to the corners when attaching this border.

Border 9 adds 12" and the quilt measures 80¾" x 90¾".

FINISHING

Layer the quilt top, batting, and backing. Baste and quilt the layers. Medallions can be simply and effectively quilted with grid or outline stitching.

Use your favorite technique to bind the layers. The binding yardage is sufficient for any method, including doublefold or bias binding.

PLANNING CHART

Use the construction and planning chart on page 95 to substitute same-sized units or to add borders to your quilt. See Planning Your Own Quilts on page 86 for detailed information on determining the number of units to use in a border and the width of spacer strips.

Peacehaven

ABOVE & BELOW: WESTMINSTER ABBEY, RESTING PLACE OF BRITISH MONARCHS AND SETTING FOR CORONATIONS AND GREAT PAGEANTS

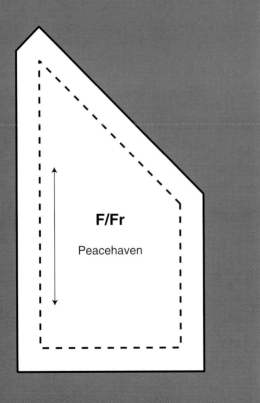

F/Fr

Peacehaven

Planning Your Own Quilts

Planning a medallion quilt is fun to do. Just follow the steps, working from the center block outward, one border at a time.

Planning Steps

CHOOSE A QUILT CENTER

First, you must decide on the center medallion block. For example, let's look at Picklescott (shown below). Its center is a 19" block. It could be any 19" block of your choice.

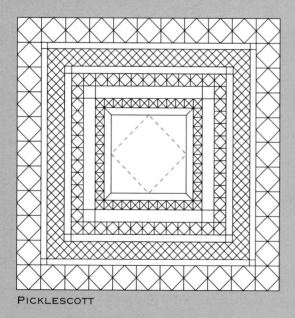

PICKLESCOTT

Just as a suggestion, any 13½" block turned on point would fill the bill. Then you would need to add triangles to the four sides to square the center. Plain border strips could be added to frame the center block and to increase the center to 22½", finished size.

As an alternate plan, you can choose any size block and frame it with a plain border, adding enough width to make the center 22½" x 22½".

ADD COMPATIBLE UNITS

The 22½" makes the center area just the right size to use the small Hour Glass units as the first pieced border. Because each Hour Glass is 2¼", you will need 10 units for each side plus four for the corners, a total of 44 units.

The finished size of the quilt top with the Hour Glass border would then be 27" x 27". Always work from and think in finished sizes for your calculations.

ADD A STRIP BORDER

The next border would be a plain strip (spacer) border, but what size? Let's skip over it for a moment while we select the next pieced border, a small Framed Square, with a finished size of 3".

If we divide the finished size of the unit into the finished size of the quilt, so far, it comes out an even nine repeats or units (27" ÷ 3" = 9 units). So we could add nine framed squares to each side without a spacer.

But let's say we want a spacer. If we use 10 Framed Squares, the spacer width needed would be 1½" finished, which would make the center area measure 30".

That seems too small, so let's use 11 Framed Squares. Then the spacer needed would be 3" wide, and the center would measure 33" before the Framed Square border is added.

For a 33" center, we would need 11 Framed Squares for each side plus four units for the corners, a total of 48 units. With the Framed Square border, the quilt would measure 39" finished.

SELECT ANOTHER PIECED BORDER

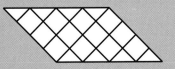

Again, skip past the next strip border for a moment and consider Triple Squares for the next pieced border. Two separate measurements need to be taken into account for Bar, Double-Square, and Triple-Square borders. The primary one is the measurement that each unit contributes to the border length. We know that net addition is 2⅛" per unit.

If we divide the quilt size of 39" by 2⅛", the result is 18.4. We have to sew whole units, so the fewest possible would be 19 units, which would leave such a narrow spacer border that we would want to go up to 20 units.

To have the correct spacer to fit 20 Triple Square units, we would need to insert a strip border 1¾" wide. After the strip border is added, the center panel will measure 42½", finished size.

We will need 20 Triple Square units per side, or 80 units, and to turn the corners, we need four Triple-Square turning units.

Now we need to consider that second measurement, the addition to the size of the quilt when we add Triple Squares. The width added to each side of the quilt is 4¼". With this border added, the center panel should measure 51" (finished).

ADD THE LAST BORDER

Our final pieced border will be the larger Framed Square, the 6" size. Again, let's skip over the strip border momentarily. Divide the quilt size of 51" by 6", and the result is 8.5.

Planning Your Own Quilts

We add only whole units, so we will have to add nine units per side. Nine times 6" equals 54", so we will need to increase the size of the center panel to 54" before we can add the Framed Squares.

Backing up to the border we skipped, that spacer strip will need to be 1½" wide to make the center panel 54" to accommodate the 6" Framed Squares.

With those 6" units added plus the 6" corners, the size of the quilt will be 66". You could substitute any 6" block for the large Framed Squares.

Now that the quilt measures 66" (finished size), feel free to add any more borders that you might want. If the last border is a plain one, it can be any width you desire. If you plan additional pieced borders, calculate the size of the spacer based on the needs of the next pieced border as discussed.

Planning Charts

We have barely scratched the surface of the number of possible quilts that can be made by using combinations of the basic styles of border treatments.

• Use the Construction Summary and Planning charts, beginning on page 90, to help you substitute same-sized units in your borders or to add borders to your quilt. The charts provide detailed information on determining the number of units to use in a border and the width of spacer strips. If you already know how to make the various units in the appropriate sizes, these charts also provide a handy summary for constructing your quilt.

• To help you in designing your own versions of classic English Medallion quilts, you will find a blank planning chart on page 102. You are welcome to photocopy it.

TILE FLOOR IN THE ENTRY OF THE BED AND BREAKFAST IN THE MALVERN AREA

Planning Your Own Quilts

While the majority of border units used in the patterned quilts were generated from 2", 3½", and 6½" squares, other triple combinations can be used. The Patches Sewn into Units charts provide some other triple patch combinations and the resulting finished sizes of various border units.

PATCHES SEWN INTO UNITS

CUT PATCH SIZES			FINISHED FRAMED SQUARE SIZES		FINISHED SAWTOOTH SIZES	
A	B	C	USE A & B	USE B & C	USE B	USE C
1½"	2½"	4½"	2"	4"	1⅝"	3⅝"
2"	3½"	6½"	3"	6"	2⅝"	5⅝"
2¼"	4"	7½"	3½"	7"	3⅛"	6⅝"
2½"	4½"	8½"	4"	8"	3⅝"	7⅝"
2¾"	5"	9½"	4½"	9"	4⅛"	8⅝"
3"	5½"	10½"	5"	10"	4⅝"	9⅝"

PATCHES SEWN INTO UNITS

CUT PATCH SIZES			FINISHED HOUR GLASS SIZES		FINISHED FLYING GEESE SIZES	
A	B	C	USE B	USE C	USE A & B	USE B & C
1½"	2½"	4½"	1¼"	3¼"	NA	1¾" x 3½"
2"	3½"	6½"	2¼"	5¼"	1¼" x 2½"	2¾" x 5½"
2¼"	4"	7½"	2¾"	6¼"	1½" x 3"	3¼" x 6½"
2½"	4½"	8½"	3¼"	7¼"	1¾" x 3½"	3¾" x 7½"
2¾"	5"	9½"	3¾"	8⅛"	2" x 4"	4¼" x 8½"
3"	5½"	10½"	4¼"	9¼"	2¼" x 4½"	4¾" x 9½"

Planning Your Own Quilts Barnard Castle

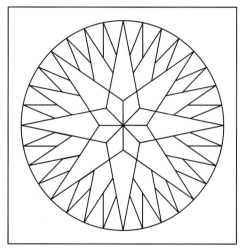

MARINER'S COMPASS BLOCK, PG. 52

BARNARD CASTLE, PG. 53

CONSTRUCTION SUMMARY AND PLANNING

QUILT TITLE:		FINISHED SIZE:		CENTER BLOCK:	
BARNARD CASTLE		**73" x 73"**		**MARINER'S COMPASS** ON POINT	

POSITION	UNIT		MAKE UNITS OR CUT STRIPS	FINISHED UNIT OR STRIP WIDTH	QUILT SIZE WITH BORDER (FINISHED)
QUILT CENTER	MARINER'S COMPASS ON POINT		1 BLOCK	28"	28" x 28"
BORDER 1	STRIP		(2) 2¼" x 28½" (2) 2¼" x 32"	1¾"	31½" x 31½"
BORDER 2	DOGTOOTH	▲	52 UNITS	2⅝"	36¾" x 36¾"
BORDER 3	STRIP		(2) 3⅛" x 42½" (2) 3⅛" x 37¼"	2⅝"	42" x 42"
BORDER 4	FRAMED SQUARE	◇	32 UNITS	6"	54" x 54"
BORDER 5 MITERED	STRIP		(4) 6⅛" x 66"	5⅝"	65¼" x 65¼"
BORDER 6	SAWTOOTH	◸	120 UNITS	2¼"	69¾" x 69¾"
BORDER 7 CORNERS	STRIP		(4) 2⅛" x 70¼" (4) 2⅛" x 2⅛"	1⅝"	73" x 73"

Planning Your Own Quilts Little Snoring

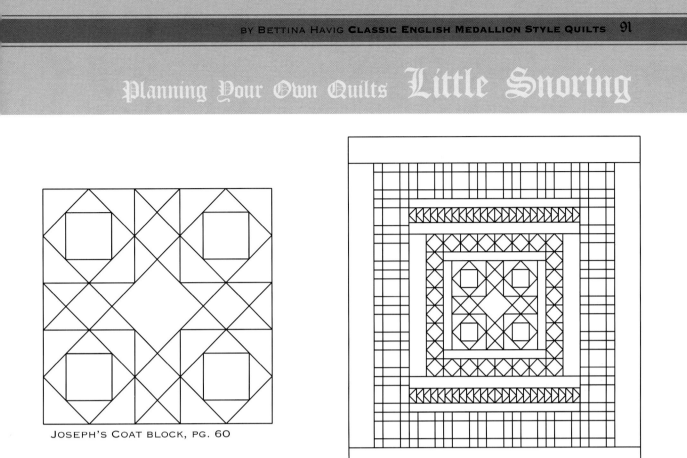

JOSEPH'S COAT BLOCK, PG. 60

LITTLE SNORING, PG. 61

CONSTRUCTION SUMMARY AND PLANNING

QUILT TITLE: LITTLE SNORING		FINISHED SIZE: 51" x 57"	CENTER BLOCK: JOSEPH'S COAT	
POSITION	**UNIT**	**MAKE UNITS OR CUT STRIPS**	**FINISHED UNIT OR STRIP WIDTH**	**QUILT SIZE WITH BORDER (FINISHED)**
QUILT CENTER	JOSEPH'S COAT	1 BLOCK	15"	15" x 15"
BORDER 1	STRIP	(2) 2" x 18½" (2) 2" x 15½"	1½"	18" x 18"
BORDER 2	FRAMED SQUARE	28 UNITS	3"	24" x 24"
BORDER 3 SIDES	STRIP	(2) 3½" x 24½"	3"	30" x 24"
TOP & BOTTOM	STRIP	(2) 2½" x 30½"	2"	30" x 28"
TOP & BOTTOM	FLYING GEESE	48 UNITS	2½"	30" x 33"
TOP & BOTTOM	STRIP	(2) 2" x 30½"	1½"	30" x 36"
BORDER 4	UNEVEN NINE-PATCH	26 UNITS	6"	42" x 48"
BORDER 5	STRIP	(2) 5" x 48½" (2) 5" x 51½"	4½"	51" x 57"

Planning Your Own Quilts Mugglewick

BRODERIE PERSE CENTER

MUGGLESWICK, PG. 31

CONSTRUCTION SUMMARY AND PLANNING

QUILT TITLE:		FINISHED SIZE:		CENTER BLOCK:
MUGGLESWICK		**68" x 68"**		**BRODERIE PERSE**

POSITION	UNIT		MAKE UNITS OR CUT STRIPS	FINISHED UNIT OR STRIP WIDTH	QUILT SIZE WITH BORDER (FINISHED)
QUILT CENTER	BRODERIE PERSE		1 BLOCK	18"	18" x 18"
BORDER 1	SAWTOOTH		36 UNITS	$2\frac{1}{4}$"	$22\frac{1}{2}$" x $22\frac{1}{2}$"
BORDER 2	STRIP		(2) 3" x 23" (2) 3" x 28"	$2\frac{1}{2}$"	$27\frac{1}{2}$" x $27\frac{1}{2}$"
BORDER 3 CORNERS	FLYING GEESE		40 UNITS (4) 6" x 6"	$5\frac{1}{2}$"	$38\frac{1}{2}$" x $38\frac{1}{2}$"
BORDER 4	STRIP		(2) $2\frac{1}{4}$" x 39" (2) $2\frac{1}{4}$" x $42\frac{1}{2}$"	$1\frac{3}{4}$"	42" x 42"
BORDER 5	FRAMED SQUARE		60 UNITS	3"	48" x 48"
BORDER 6	STRIP		(2) 2" x $48\frac{1}{2}$" (2) 2" x $51\frac{1}{2}$"	$1\frac{1}{2}$"	51" x 51"
BORDER 7	UNEVEN NINE-PATCH		28 UNITS	$8\frac{1}{2}$"	68" x 68"
BORDER 8 (OPTIONAL)	STRIP (NOT SHOWN)		(4) $6\frac{1}{2}$" x $80\frac{3}{4}$" MITERED CORNERS	6"	80" x 80"

Planning Your Own Quilts Pilgrim's Hatch

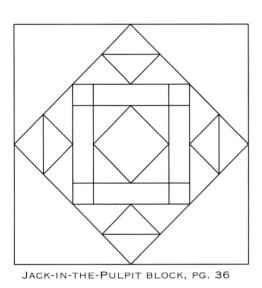

JACK-IN-THE-PULPIT BLOCK, PG. 36

PILGRIM'S HATCH, PG. 37

CONSTRUCTION SUMMARY AND PLANNING

QUILT TITLE:	FINISHED SIZE:		CENTER BLOCK:	
PILGRIM'S HATCH	**55¼" x 55¼"**		**JACK-IN-THE-PULPIT** ON POINT	
POSITION	UNIT	MAKE UNITS OR CUT STRIPS	FINISHED UNIT OR STRIP WIDTH	QUILT SIZE WITH BORDER (FINISHED)
QUILT CENTER	JACK-IN-THE-PULPIT ON POINT	1 BLOCK	12" 17"	12" x 12" 17" x 17"
BORDER 1	STRIP	(2) 1" x 17½" (2) 1" x 18½"	½"	18" x 18"
BORDER 2	FRAMED SQUARE 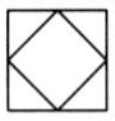	28 UNITS	3"	24" x 24"
BORDER 3	STRIP	(2) 3" x 24½" (2) 3" x 29½"	2½"	29" x 29"
BORDER 4	SAWTOOTH 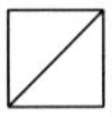	48 UNITS	2⅝"	34¼" x 34¼"
BORDER 5	STRIP	(2) 2½" x 34¾" (2) 2½" x 38¾"	2"	38¼" x 38¼"
BORDER 6 CORNERS	TRIPLE SQUARE 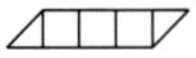	72 UNITS 4 TURNING UNITS	4¼"	46¾" x 46¾"
BORDER 7	STRIP	(2) 4¾" x 47¼" (2) 4¾" x 55¾"	4¼"	55¼" x 55¼"

Planning Your Own Quilts

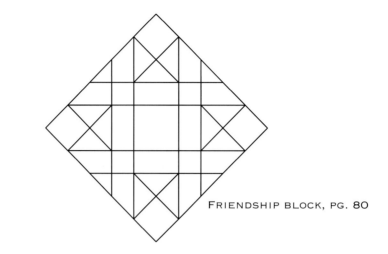

FRIENDSHIP BLOCK, PG. 80

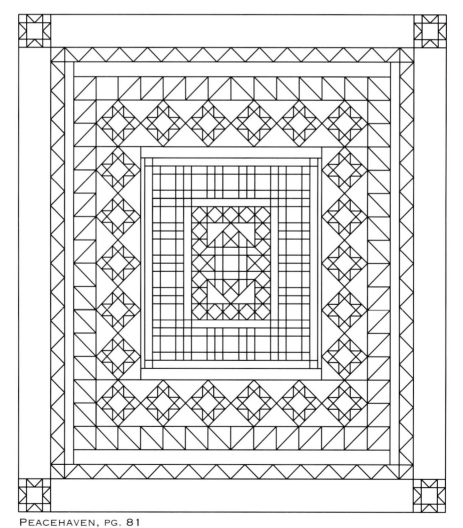

PEACEHAVEN, PG. 81

Peacehaven

CONSTRUCTION SUMMARY AND PLANNING

QUILT TITLE: **PEACEHAVEN**	FINISHED SIZE: **80¼" x 90¼"**		CENTER BLOCK: **FRIENDSHIP** ON POINT	
POSITION	**UNIT**	**MAKE UNITS OR CUT STRIPS**	**FINISHED UNIT OR STRIP WIDTH**	**QUILT SIZE WITH BORDER (FINISHED)**
QUILT CENTER	FRIENDSHIP ON POINT WITH FRAME	10½" (APPROX.) 15" x 21"	15" x 21"	15" x 21"
BORDER 1 CORNERS	STRIP	(2) 2" x 15½" (2) 2" x 21½" (4) 2" x 2"	1½"	18" x 24"
BORDER 2	UNEVEN NINE-PATCH 	18 UNITS	6"	30" x 36"
BORDER 3 CORNERS	STRIP	(2) 2" x 30½" (2) 2" x 36½" (4) 2" x 2"	1½"	33" x 39"
BORDER 4 TOP & BOTTOM SIDES	STRIP STRIP	(2) 2" x 34½" (2) 1" x 39½"	1½" ½"	33" x 42" 34" x 42"
BORDER 5	EVENING STAR ON POINT 	22 UNITS	8½"	51" x 59"
BORDER 6	SAWTOOTH 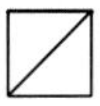	56 UNITS	4¼"	59½" x 67½"
BORDER 7 TOP & BOTTOM SIDES	STRIP STRIP	(2) 3¼" x 60" (2) 2¼" x 73½"	2¾" 1¾"	59½" x 73" 63" x 73"
BORDER 8 CORNERS	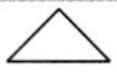 DOGTOOTH SAWTOOTH	100 UNITS 4 UNITS	2⅝"	68¼" x 78¼"
BORDER 9 CORNERS	STRIP EVENING STAR	(2) 6½" x 68¾" (2) 6½" x 78¾" 4 UNITS	6"	80¼" x 90¼"

Planning Your Own Quilts Rainbow Hill

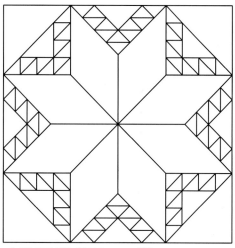

LUCINDA'S STAR, PG. 66

RAINBOW HILL, PG. 67

CONSTRUCTION SUMMARY AND PLANNING

QUILT TITLE:		FINISHED SIZE:		CENTER BLOCK:
RAINBOW HILL		**72" x 72"**		**LUCINDA'S STAR**

POSITION	UNIT		MAKE UNITS OR CUT STRIPS	FINISHED UNIT OR STRIP WIDTH	QUILT SIZE WITH BORDER (FINISHED)
QUILT CENTER	LUCINDA'S STAR		1 BLOCK	18"	18" x 18"
BORDER 1	SAWTOOTH		40 UNITS	2"	22" x 22"
BORDER 2	STRIP		(4) 3" x 22½"	2½"	27" x 27"
BORDER 3	HOUR GLASS		52 UNITS	2¼"	31½" x 31½"
BORDER 4 CORNERS	BAR		60 UNITS 4 TURNING UNITS	3⅛"	37¾" x 37¾"
BORDER 5 MITERED	STRIP		(4) 2⅝" x 42¾"	2⅛"	42" x 42"
BORDER 6	FRAMED SQUARE		60 UNITS	3"	48" x 48"
BORDER 7	FRAMED SQUARE		36 UNITS	6"	60" x 60"
BORDER 8 MITERED	STRIP		(4) 6½" x 72¾"	6"	72" x 72"

Planning Your Own Quilts Wigglesworth

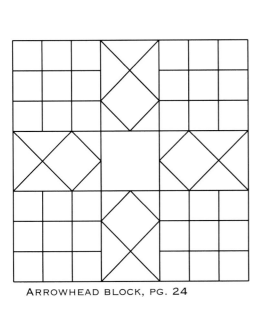

ARROWHEAD BLOCK, PG. 24

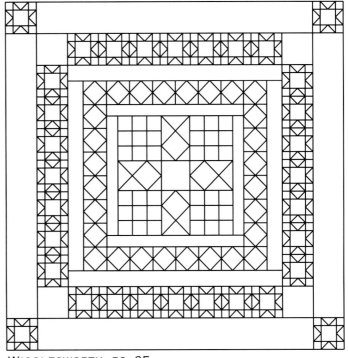

WIGGLESWORTH, PG. 25

CONSTRUCTION SUMMARY AND PLANNING

QUILT TITLE:	FINISHED SIZE:	CENTER BLOCK:
WIGGLESWORTH	**44" x 44"**	**ARROWHEAD**

POSITION	UNIT	MAKE UNITS OR CUT STRIPS	FINISHED UNIT OR STRIP WIDTH	QUILT SIZE WITH BORDER (FINISHED)
QUILT CENTER	ARROWHEAD	1 BLOCK	15"	15" x 15"
BORDER 1	STRIP	(2) 2" x 15½" (2) 2" x 18½"	1½"	18" x 18"
BORDER 2	FRAMED SQUARE	28 UNITS	3"	24" x 24"
BORDER 3	STRIP	(2) 2½" x 24½" (2) 2½" x 28½"	2"	28" x 28"
BORDER 4 CORNERS	EVENING STAR	28 UNITS (4) 4" x 4"	4"	36" x 36"
BORDER 5 CORNERS	STRIP EVENING STAR	(4) 4½" x 36½" 4 UNITS	4" 4"	44" x 44"

Planning Your Own Quilts

BRODERIE PERSE CENTER

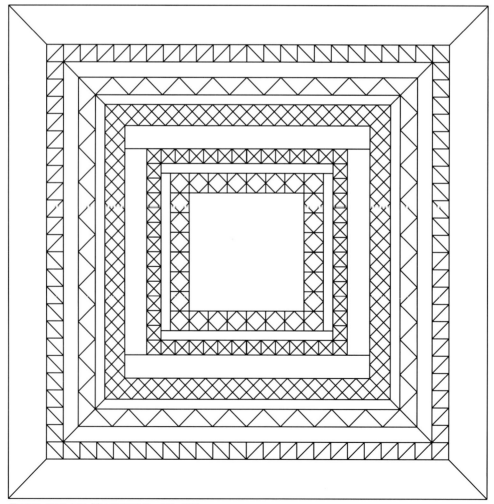

REST AND BE THANKFUL, PG. 75

Rest & Be Thankful

CONSTRUCTION SUMMARY AND PLANNING

QUILT TITLE:	FINISHED SIZE:	CENTER BLOCK:
REST AND BE THANKFUL	**75" x 75"**	**BRODERIE PERSE**

POSITION	UNIT	MAKE UNITS OR CUT STRIPS	FINISHED UNIT OR STRIP WIDTH	QUILT SIZE WITH BORDER (FINISHED)
QUILT CENTER	*BRODERIE PERSE*	1 BLOCK	18"	18" x 18"
BORDER 1	FRAMED SQUARE	28 UNITS	3"	24" x 24"
BORDER 2	STRIP	(2) 2" x 24½" (2) 2" x 27½"	1½"	27" x 27"
BORDER 3	HOUR GLASS	52 UNITS	2¼"	31½" x 31½"
BORDER 4	STRIP	(2) 3¾" x 32" (2) 3¾" x 38½"	3¼"	38" x 38"
BORDER 5 CORNERS	DOUBLE SQUARE	72 UNITS 4 TURNING UNITS	3⅛"	44¼" x 44¼"
BORDER 6 MITERED	STRIP	(4) 2" x 48"	1½"	47¼" x 47¼"
BORDER 7	DOGTOOTH	76 UNITS	2⅝"	52½" x 52½"
BORDER 8 MITERED	STRIP	(4) 3⅛" x 58½"	2⅝"	57¾" x 57¾"
BORDER 9	SAWTOOTH	92 UNITS	2⅝"	63" x 63"
BORDER 10 MITERED	STRIP	(4) 6½" x 75¾"	6"	75" x 75"

Planning Your Own Quilts

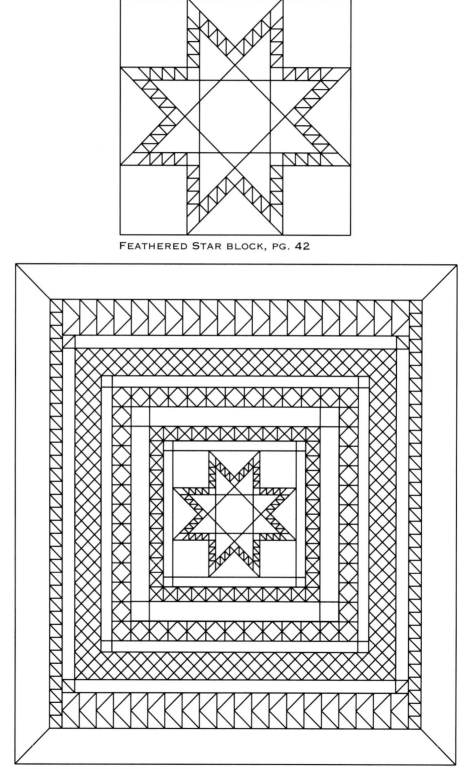

FEATHERED STAR BLOCK, PG. 42

SCARBOROUGH FAIRE, PG. 43

Scarborough Faire

CONSTRUCTION SUMMARY AND PLANNING

QUILT TITLE:		FINISHED SIZE:	CENTER BLOCK:
SCARBOROUGH FAIRE		**70" X 77"**	**FEATHERED STAR**

POSITION	UNIT	MAKE UNITS OR CUT STRIPS	FINISHED UNIT OR STRIP WIDTH	QUILT SIZE WITH BORDER (FINISHED)
QUILT CENTER	FEATHERED STAR	1 BLOCK	19½"	19½" x 19½"
BORDER 1 CORNERS	STRIP	(4) 2" x 20" (4) 2" x 2"	1½" 1½"	22½" x 22½"
BORDER 2	HOUR GLASS 	44 UNITS	2¼"	27" x 27"
BORDER 3 CORNERS	STRIP	(4) 3½" x 27½" (4) 3½" x 3½"	3"	33" x 33"
BORDER 4	FRAMED SQUARE 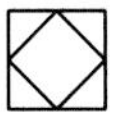	48 UNITS	3"	39" x 39"
BORDER 5 CORNERS	STRIP	(4) 2¼" x 39½" (4) 2¼" x 2¼"	1¾"	42½" x 42½"
BORDER 6 CORNERS	TRIPLE SQUARE 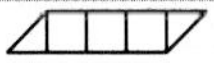	80 UNITS 4 TURNING UNITS	4¼"	51" x 51"
BORDER 7 CORNERS	STRIP SAWTOOTH 	(4) 2½" x 51½" 4 UNITS	2" 2"	55" x 55"
BORDER 8 TOP & BOTTOM SIDES	FLYING GEESE 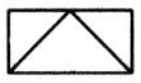 SAWTOOTH 	40 UNITS 66 UNITS	5½" 2"	55" x 66" 59" x 66"
BORDER 9 MITERED	STRIP	(2) 6" x 70¾" (2) 6" x 77¾"	5½"	70" x 77"

Planning Your Own Quilts

CONSTRUCTION SUMMARY AND PLANNING

QUILT TITLE: FINISHED SIZE: CENTER BLOCK:

POSITION	UNIT	MAKE UNITS OR CUT STRIPS	FINISHED UNIT OR STRIP WIDTH	QUILT SIZE WITH BORDER (FINISHED)
QUILT CENTER				
BORDER 1				
BORDER 2				
BORDER 3				
BORDER 4				
BORDER 5				
BORDER 6				
BORDER 7				
BORDER 8				
BORDER 9				
BORDER 10				

PLEASE COPY THIS CHART AS NEEDED FOR PLANNING YOUR OWN MEDALLION STYLE QUILTS.

Three More Quilts

The last three quilt plans are left for you to complete: Giggleswick (pages 104–105), Banbury Cross (pages 106–108), and Picklescott (page 109). Make your own decisions about fabric, yardage, and even substitute a different center block, if you like. Don't worry about computing yardage — you can always supplement with new fabrics and just make the scrap-look more interesting.

PAY-TO-USE PUBLIC PARK IN BATH

Giggleswick

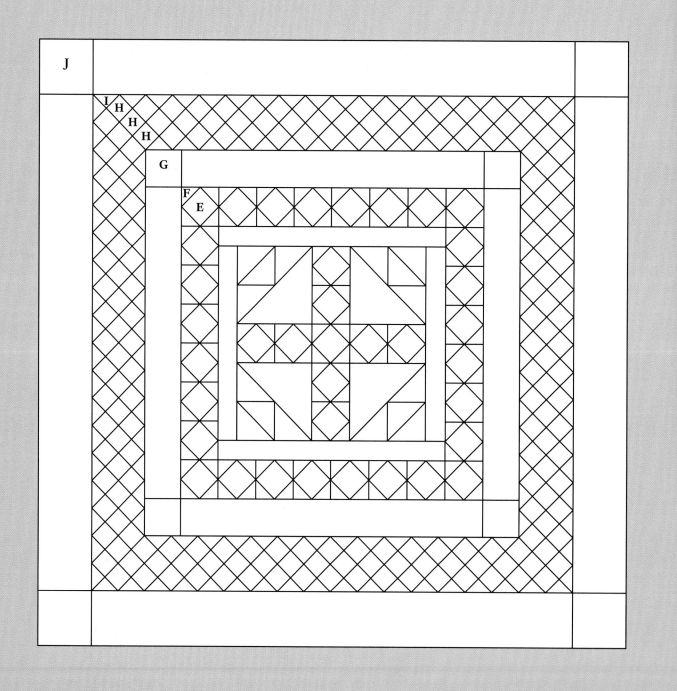

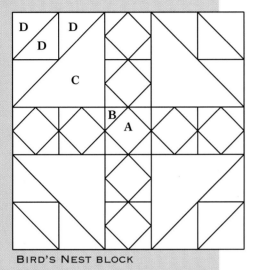

BIRD'S NEST BLOCK

Bird's Nest block
rotary cutting

9 A   2⅝" x 2⅝"

18 B   2⅜" x 2⅜", cut once diagonally to make 36 half-square triangles

2 C   6⅞" x 6⅞", cut once diagonally to make 4 half-square triangles

8 D   3⅞" x 3⅞", cut once diagonally to make 16 half-square triangles

CONSTRUCTION SUMMARY AND PLANNING

QUILT TITLE:		FINISHED SIZE:		CENTER BLOCK:
GIGGLESWICK		**46¾" x 46¾"**		**BIRD'S NEST**

POSITION	UNIT	MAKE UNITS OR CUT STRIPS	FINISHED UNIT OR STRIP WIDTH	QUILT SIZE WITH BORDER (FINISHED)
QUILT CENTER	BIRD'S NEST	1 BLOCK	15"	15" x 15"
BORDER 1	STRIP	(2) 2" x 15½" (2) 2" x 18½"	1½"	18" x 18"
BORDER 2	FRAMED SQUARE	28 UNITS	3"	24" x 24"
BORDER 3 CORNERS	STRIP	(4) 3⅜" x 24½" (4) 3⅜" x 3⅜"	2⅞"	29¾" x 29¾"
BORDER 4 CORNERS	TRIPLE SQUARE	56 UNITS 4 TURNING UNITS	4¼"	38¼" x 38¼"
BORDER 5 CORNERS	STRIP	(4) 4¾" x 38¾" (4) 4¾" x 4¾"	4¼"	46¾" x 46¾"

Banbury Cross

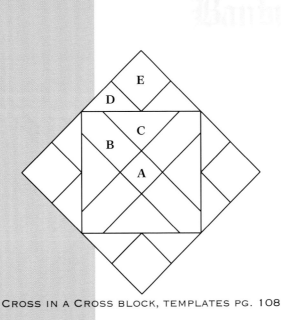

CROSS IN A CROSS BLOCK, TEMPLATES PG. 108

CONSTRUCTION SUMMARY AND PLANNING

QUILT TITLE:		FINISHED SIZE:		CENTER BLOCK:
BANBURY CROSS		**80" X 80"**		**CROSS IN A CROSS** ON POINT

POSITION	UNIT	MAKE UNITS OR CUT STRIPS	FINISHED UNIT OR STRIP WIDTH	QUILT SIZE WITH BORDER (FINISHED)
QUILT CENTER	CROSS IN A CROSS ON POINT	1 BLOCK	10" 14"	14" X 14"
BORDER 1 CORNERS	STRIP	(4) 4" x 14½" (4) 4" x 4"	3½"	21" X 21"
BORDER 2	SAWTOOTH	36 UNITS	2⅝"	26¼" X 26¼"
BORDER 3 CORNERS	STRIP	(4) 3⅛" x 26¾" (4) 3⅛" x 3⅛"	2⅝"	31½" X 31½"
BORDER 4	SAWTOOTH	52 UNITS	2⅝"	36¾" X 36¾"
BORDER 5 CORNERS	STRIP	(4) 3⅛" x 37¼" (4) 3⅛" x 3⅛"	2⅝"	42" X 42"
BORDER 6	FRAMED SQUARE	60 UNITS	3"	48" X 48"
BORDER 7 CORNERS	STRIP	(2) 3½" x 48½" (4) 3½" x 3½"	3"	54" X 54"
BORDER 8	UNEVEN NINE-PATCH	40 UNITS	6"	66" X 66"
BORDER 9 MITERED	STRIP	(4) 7½" x 80¾"	7"	80" X 80"

Banbury Cross

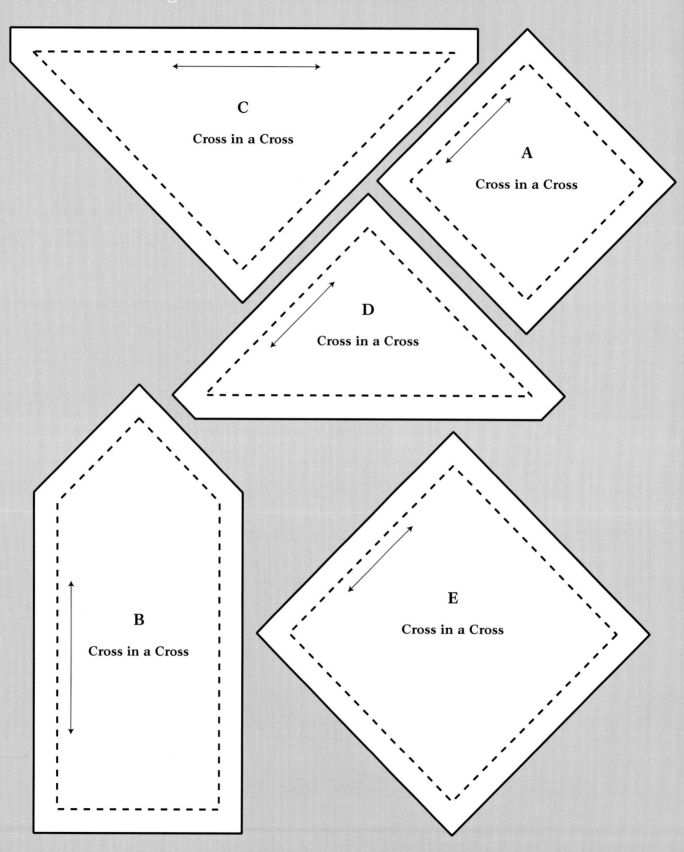

C
Cross in a Cross

A
Cross in a Cross

D
Cross in a Cross

B
Cross in a Cross

E
Cross in a Cross

Picklescott

A 13½" BLOCK ON POINT CAN BE USED IN THE 19" CENTER.

CONSTRUCTION SUMMARY AND PLANNING

QUILT TITLE:		FINISHED SIZE:	CENTER BLOCK:	
PICKLESCOTT		**66" x 66"**	**MAKER'S CHOICE, 19" BLOCK**	

POSITION	UNIT	MAKE UNITS OR CUT STRIPS	FINISHED UNIT OR STRIP WIDTH	QUILT SIZE WITH BORDER (FINISHED)
QUILT CENTER	YOUR CHOICE	1 BLOCK	19"	19" x 19"
BORDER 1 MITERED	STRIP	(4) 2¼" x 23¼"	1¾"	22½" x 22½"
BORDER 2	HOUR GLASS	44 UNITS	2¼"	27" x 27"
BORDER 3 CORNERS	STRIP	(4) 3½" x 33½" (4) 3½" x 3½"	3"	33" x 33"
BORDER 4	FRAMED SQUARES	48 UNITS	3"	39" x 39"
BORDER 5 CORNERS	STRIP	(4) 2¼" x 39½" (4) 2¼" x 2¼"	1¾"	42½" x 42½"
BORDER 6 CORNERS	TRIPLE SQUARE	80 UNITS 4 TURNING UNITS	4¼"	51" x 51"
BORDER 7 CORNERS	STRIP	(4) 2" x 51½" (4) 2" x 2"	1½"	54" x 54"
BORDER 8	FRAMED SQUARES	40 UNITS	6"	66" x 66"

Bibliography

Allen, Rosemary E. *North Country Quilts and Coverlets from the Beamish Museum*. County Durham: Beamish Museum, 1987.

Averil, Colby. *Patchwork Quilts*. 1965. Reprint, London: B.T. Batsford Ltd., 1988.

Meldrum, Alex, curator. *Irish Patchwork, Kilkenny, Ireland*. Design Workshop Ltd., 1979. An exhibition catalog.

Osler, Dorothy. *North Country Quilts*. Friends of the Bowes Museum, 2000.

Osler, Dorothy. *Traditional British Quilts*. London: B.T. Batsford Ltd., 1987.

Quilt Treasures of Great Britain: The Heritage Search of the Quilters' Guild. Rutledge Hill Press, 1995.

Rae, Janet. *The Quilts of the British Isles*. E.P. Dutton, 1987.

TOWN FOUNTAIN AT CAMBRIDGE WITH MARKET STALLS IN THE BACKGROUND

About the Author

Bettina Havig wears many hats. Since learning to quilt in 1970, she has immersed herself in the quilt world, taken on many challenges, and become a quilt appraiser, quilt show judge, quilt historian, quiltmaker, and consultant. She shares her love for quilting with others by teaching, lecturing, and writing, and she has appeared as a guest on HGTV's *Simply Quilts* (episode #525). Teaching has given her a chance to travel to Germany, Scotland, and England, where her love of traditional English medallion-style quilts was born.

In her capacity as a quilt historian, she has been an active member of the American Quilt Study Group (AQSG) since 1980 and currently serves as president. She represents AQSG on the advisory board of the International Quilt Study Center in Lincoln, Nebraska, and is a board member for the Museum of the American Quilter's Society (MAQS), in Paducah, Kentucky.

Her experience as a quilt historian took her to new levels when she served as guest curator for the SITES (Smithsonian Institution Traveling Exhibit Service) exhibit, Women of Taste, for its premiere at Silver Dollar City, Missouri, in the fall of 1999.

She is also known for her design skills. In 2001, she designed a series of patterns for *British Patchwork and Quilting* magazine. She has received invitations to exhibit her quilts in a number of national quilt shows, and her quilts have twice appeared in the AQS *Quilt Art Engagement Calendar*. She has quilts in both private and corporate collections.

She has authored five books: *Missouri Heritage Quilts* (AQS, 1986), *Amish Quiltmaker* (Sterling, 1992), *Quilts of the Booneslick Trail Quilters' Guild* (ASN, 1994), *Amish Kinder Komforts* (AQS, 1996), and *Carrie Hall Blocks* (AQS, 1999).

Other AQS Books

This is only a small selection of the books available from the American Quilter's Society. AQS books are known worldwide for timely topics, clear writing, beautiful color photos, and accurate illustrations and patterns. The following books are available from your local bookseller, quilt shop, or public library:

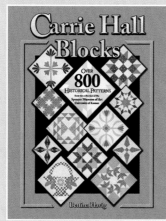

#4957   us$34.95

#6210   us$24.95

#6074   us$21.95

#6293   us$24.95

#6212   us$25.95

us$21.95

#6076   us$21.95

#6208   us$24.95

#6078   us$19.95

#5756   us$19.95

LOOK for these books nationally. CALL or VISIT our website at www.AQSquilt.com.

1-800-626-5420